The DIY Bride

Crafty Countdown

40 Fabulous Projects to Make in the Months,

Weeks & Hours before Your Special Day

Khris Cochran

A Stonesong Press Book

The Taunton Press

The Taunton Press
Inspiration for hands-on living®

The Taunton Press, Inc., 63 South Main Street, PO Box 5506, Newtown, CT 06470-5506
e-mail: tp@taunton.com

Editor: Courtney Jordan
Copy editor: Candace B. Levy
Indexer: Lynne Lipkind
Jacket/Cover design: 3&Co.
Cover and Chapter opener illustration: Asami Yamazaki and Meredith Harte Londagin/3&Co.
Interior design: 3&Co.
Layout: 3&Co.
Illustrator: woolypear
Photographer: Jack Deutsch
Stylist: Laura Maffeo
A Stonesong Press Book

Library of Congress Cataloging-in-Publication Data
Cochran, Khris.
  The DIY bride crafty countdown : 40 fabulous projects to make in the months, weeks & hours before your special day / Khris Cochran.
    p. cm.
  Includes index.
  ISBN 978-1-60085-119-3
  1. Handicraft. 2. Wedding decorations. I. Title.
  TT149.C5835 2009
  745.5--dc22
                              2009033523

Printed in the United States of America
10 9 8 7 6 5 4 3 2

The following names/manufacturers appearing in *DIY Bride Crafty Countdown* are trademarks: Action Envelope℠, Addicted to Rubber Stamps®, Autumn Leaves®, Bakelite®, Bunco®, Chatterbox, Inc.℠, Clipart.com™, Copic®, Crate & Barrel®, Crayola®, Cristal®, Cuisinart®, Cuttlebug™, Dick Blick℠, eBay®, Flowerbud.com®, Food Network®, Grower's Box℠, Home Depot℠, Ikea®, iStockphoto®, Jo-Ann Fabric and Craft Stores℠, KI® Memories, Lowe's℠, The Memory Box®, Michaels Stores℠, Microsoft®Word, Paper Mart℠, Paper Source℠, Rockler®, Samuel Adams®, Silpat®, Stampin' Up!®, The Ribbon Spot™, Vespa®, West Elm®, X-ACTO™

Dedication

My everlasting love and gratitude go to my amazing husband, Jason, for being my tireless cheerleader, my dedicated and loving partner, and an incredible dad to our beautiful son, Zion, who was born during the making of this book.

Acknowledgments

This book would not have been possible without the endless and extraordinary support of the most awesome team I could ever have hoped for. The team members from The Stonesong Press—Alison Fargis, Katie Feiereisel, and Ellen Scordato—truly deserve some kind of medal for their work on this book. Their never-ending patience, genuine kindness, and adaptability when things went awry—and, oh boy, did things ever go wonky!—helped me keep my sanity throughout the journey of creating this book. I am deeply indebted to them for the endless hand-holding and above-and-beyond efforts to make this book happen. There are few people in this industry as creative and delightful as my photographer, Jack Deutsch, and stylist, Laura Maffeo. Their extraordinary talents took the projects in this book and showcased them as pieces of wedding art. And, of course, I must wholeheartedly thank Erica Sanders-Foege and Courtney Jordan, my editors at The Taunton Press, for believing in *The DIY Bride* and giving me the opportunity to create this book. Their gentle guidance, sound advice, and fantastic editorial skills have made me a better writer and a more detail-oriented crafter. The outstanding quality of this book is due to their efforts, and I am forever grateful.

Please Save The Date

October 10, 2010

For Tina & Mark's Wedding

In The Beautiful Forests Of

Yosemite National Park

Details To Follow

Katerina
&
Vincent

Together with their parents

Isabella Valenchez

and

Craig McDonnell

request the honour of your presence

at their marriage

on Saturday, the 10th of August

Two thousand and ten

at six o'clock in the evening

Unity Church

12545 Main Street

Pasadena, California

Dear Eric & Ellen,

Contents

Introduction

You, my delightfully sophisticated and cosmopolitan friends, are busy. You've got up-and-coming careers, full social calendars, myriad family obligations, a brand new engagement, and now a wedding to plan and crafts aplenty to make. How are you possibly going to do it all? Don't worry. I've got your backs.

See, I've been there. In October 2000, I pulled off—after much blood, sweat, and tears spilled at my kitchen table—my own crafty wedding. In those days, there weren't many resources for do-it-yourself weddings, and I was totally flying by the seat of my pants. I didn't know much about weddings, and I knew even less about the big world of crafting. Most of the crafty moves I know now came from simple trial and error (emphasis on *error* here, kids—I am not as clever as I like to think I am) during that time. My mission in the years after my wedding—and the hundreds of weddings I've helped with since then—has been to tell the tale of how to get through the crafting bits with your relationship, budget, and sanity all (mostly) intact. The most common problem do-it-yourselfers get

themselves into is vastly underestimating the time it takes to plan, design, and complete a project.

Please repeat after me: "I promise not to be a crafty procrastinator." The last thing you want to do the night before your wedding is assemble 200 favors or sew 100 programs. Yes, dear bride-to-be, I was once that girl.

Add this DIY trip-up with timing to the natural chaos that is wedding planning and things can go a little haywire, creating stress and frustration—two things every couple needs way less of when contemplating the most awesome event in their lives to date!

Enter *The DIY Bride Crafty Countdown*, my one-of-a-kind timeline that gives you all the tools you need to plan and execute your one-of-a-kind wedding.

You're a resourceful lady, so I know you've seen wedding timelines before. They are exceedingly helpful and, I argue, absolutely necessary for keeping you on track (and relatively sane) during the planning process. However, those run-of-the mill versions fall short for fabulous brides like you. They're so . . . generic. How could they possibly inspire someone who's planning a 1930s Shanghai-inspired soiree? Or delightful couples who are trekking to lands far and away for a once-in-a-life-time wedding in the African savanna? You deserve better, baby. Lucky for you, *The DIY Bride Crafty Countdown* takes the timeline to the oh-so-awe-some next level by organizing your wedding around fabulous crafts. That means I'll get you organized from the earliest stages of your wedding project planning right down to those last precious hours before you walk down the aisle. This book is *the* essential guide to getting your personalized and perfectly gorgeous wedding done right—on time, on or under budget, and without meltdowns. What could be better?

I cover everything the bride in you will need, from the essentials (save-the-dates, invites, favors, and thank-yous) to the little details (like stamped cocktail napkins and oh-so-stunning bridal slippers) that will make your wedding uniquely *you*. Along the way, I'll be sharing helpful hints on who should help out, tips for completing the projects, great ways to add your own innovative touches, and nifty resources section for finding those not-so-obvious supplies.

As you're probably painfully aware, weddings are obnoxiously expensive these days. Let me dispel the notion that having an awesome wedding means spending big bucks. Wrong, wrong, wrong! Throw-ing cash at random wedding swag doesn't make a wedding more memorable or worthy of praise. No, what makes a wedding special and worthwhile are well-chosen and well-crafted elements that reflect the personalities of the couple. The DIY Bride philosophy has always been that anyone can have an amazing wedding no matter her finances. The beauty of the projects I've included in this book is that they're all adaptable to nearly any style and budget while still looking like a million bucks. Just check out how little you have to spend in the Crafty Calculator sidebar at the end of each project and then compare it to what you'd have to pay else-where to get the same great items in the Cost Comparison section! So with a little effort on your part, you can contribute creative, stylish, and money-wise elements to your wedding that are truly meaningful (and won't send you into sticker shock). And that's priceless.

The projects in these pages are designed for crafters and would-be crafters of all skill levels. Whether you're new to the scene or are sporting a hand-sewn, bejeweled hot glue gun holster, I promise that you can turn out crafts that rival anything you'll find in the pages of a bridal mag. Why spend a hundred bucks or more on a jeweled bridal headband when you can make your own—in mere minutes—for around $20? Who needs to rent an overpriced photo booth when you can create a totally unique photo stage area that'll have your guests talking for years to come? I'll show you how! And with *The DIY Bride Crafty Countdown's* easy-breezy Project Planning Sheet, you'll have no problem prepping for your projects, staying on task, or keeping your supplies straight.

I know you're style conscious, and you know I adore you for that, right? With you in mind, the projects in this book are designed to be crafty chameleons. They can be dressed up or down to fit your distinctive vision. Sophisticated and modern?

Go for it. Retro whimsy? Yep, you can do that, too. Classic or preppy or vintage or themed? Of course. A mix of all of the above? No problem! Let your imagination go wild. Make these creations truly yours, and if you need a little crafty guidance, look in the Tips & Hints section I've included for every project. You'll find stellar ways to change up each item to make it reflect awesome you.

And the bottom line is a girl's gotta splurge on a few special touches for her big day, and *The DIY Bride Crafty Countdown* lets you indulge without the guilt! I don't mean conspicuous consumption here. Ditch those forgettable tchotchkes for things that you, your family, and your friends will love for years to come. Turn a grandmother's crocheted doily into a special keepsake by transforming it into an heirloom flower girl's basket. Raiding a beloved auntie's jewelry box can yield swanky jewels to adorn your 100 percent one-of-a-kind bridal slippers, which will be in your wardrobe forever and ever. With all of the savings you'll get by going DIY, you can put your precious pennies toward that top-notch caterer, that to-die-for dress, or an award-winning photographer, an upgraded honeymoon, or even a down payment on your dream home!

View *The DIY Bride Crafty Countdown* as a way to put your personal mark on your wedding and save plenty while you are at it. The projects in this book are designed to be stylish, fun, adaptable to your tastes, and easy on the piggy bank—that's a win–win for any bride-to-be!

As someone who looks for any excuse to entertain friends and family, making a craft project into a party-worthy event really excites me—and I hope it does you, too. Wedding planning plus crafting equals great times that deserve to be shared. Your friends and family, utterly fabulous as they are, are often eager to help you out with your wedding stuff. Take them up on it! Each project in the book suggests who to invite over for a little craft time and offers swell party suggestions for keeping it fun and light.

While I can't take away all of the chaos and stress of wedding planning, I hope these pages can show you just how doable having a smashing, personal, and creative do-it-yourself wedding can be. With this book as your guide, you'll have your wedding planned to the last crafty detail in no time flat, save big bucks, and have more fun than you could possibly imagine bringing your big day to life. So what are you waiting for?

Let the Crafty Countdown begin!

The Basics

As a newbie crafter—or as a seasoned one attempting a brand new technique—the unfamiliar can be quite intimidating. Don't despair! Being the great pal that I am, I wouldn't think of setting you loose on the projects in this book without helping you with the basics. The following is a quick guide to the essential tools and techniques you'll need to create the projects in this book just like a pro.

If you're like most gals in the midst of planning a wedding, you're on a tight budget, but rest assured, my dear DIY Bride, the tools and supplies used in this book have a long crafty life beyond just your wedding and reception. You'll find yourself creating variations on the projects herein for years to come, for everything from dinner parties and birthdays to holidays and special events. I promise that everything in this guide gives big bang for your crafty buck!

Must-Have Tools & Supplies

The handy-dandy tools I introduce here will make any of your craft projects more gorgeous, elegant, and utterly fab than they already are! They range from supplies every crafter should have in her toolbox, such as double-sided tape, a hot glue gun, stamps and ink pads, and scissors, to more specialized tools, like the Cuttlebug™ and Crop-A-Dile. Check out the Resources (p. 214) for my tips and hints on where to find everything.

Adhesives

Double-sided tape: For quick and easy bonding, use clear tape that has adhesive on both sides. It provides an instant bond and will not bleed through or buckle paper. Use it instead of glue on paper projects.

Fabric glue: No sewing experience? No problem! Fabric glue, a liquid adhesive, is perfect for permanent fabric-to-fabric bonds. It dries stiff but can be softened with a warm iron without losing its hold.

Glue gun & glue sticks: Trigger-fed glue guns heat solid glue sticks and dispense the melted glue. The glue has an instant bond and is perfect for adhering nonpaper craft materials like silk flowers, lace, and ribbon. But be careful, hot glue will sometimes bleed through lighter-weight paper.

Red line tape: When paper projects require an extra-strength bond, red line tape is a must. It's a heavier version of regular double-sided tape with a translucent red liner that peels off on one side.

Spray adhesive: One of my favorite adhesives for crafting is spray adhesive, an aerosol glue. It's best used for adhering paper to paper or paper to fabric. It creates a permanent bond, adheres very quickly, and dries clear. Always use it in a well-ventilated space.

Cutting tools

Craft knife: One brand of craft knife is X-Acto™, and this sharp, single-edged knife has a pencil-like handle. It's best for cutting ornate designs on paper, vellum, and other thin materials. Heavy-duty versions are also available for cutting thicker materials like chipboard and balsa wood.

Cutting mat: Self-healing cutting mats are often used with craft knives and rotary cutters. The surface repairs itself after a cut, leaving a smooth cutting area for your next project. Most feature ruled lines on the face to make measuring and cutting a snap.

Paper cutter: Use a paper cutter for making straight cuts on individual pieces of paper and card stock. Most styles have either a simple sliding blade or a rotary blade with built-in measuring grids or rulers.

Rotary cutter: A rotary cutter looks and acts much like a pizza wheel. It cuts fabric or paper as it rolls over the surface. This allows you to make a long, straight cut in a single movement.

Scissors: A good pair of general-purpose scissors is a must for any crafter. Invest in the best pair you can buy within your budget. Stainless-steel blades will last decades with minimum maintenance. A 5- to 8-in. blade will be suitable for most crafts.

Rubber stamps

Add graphics to craft projects by using art stamps. There are two common types of stamps on the market: rubber and acrylic. Rubber stamps are opaque; acrylic stamps are transparent. Both will imprint images, words, or patterns on nearly any surface and are available in numerous designs and sizes.

Inks

To use a rubber stamp, you've got to have an ink pad. There are thousands of colors available from a number of manufacturers. Although there are several types of inks to choose from, there are two kinds that will carry you through the majority of your stamp projects.

Dye inks: Dye-based inks are water-based, permanent inks. They dry quickly and can be used on any kind of paper. But because of their fast drying time, they are not suitable for embossing.

Pigment inks: Pigment inks are thicker and come in more vibrant colors than dye inks. They also take longer to dry. Just like dye inks, they can be used on any kind of paper, but will smudge when wet. Because of their slow drying time, they are great to use with embossing powders.

Heating tools

Heat embossing tool: A handy gadget is a heat embossing tool; reminiscent of a hair dryer, it can be used to melt wax. It can also be used to melt embossing powders on your paper crafts.

Wood burning tool: Ideal for decorating wood veneer, a wood burning tool can also be used to add images to paper, leather, and, yes, wood!

Working with wire

Wire cutters: Good wire cutters are essential for all wire projects. They can bend wire, twist closures, and leave a smooth edge when it comes time to clipping ends. Like a good pair of scissors, they'll last for years and require little maintenance.

Paper crafts

Bone folder: Bone folders are used to smooth, score, and crease paper. Traditionally, they're made of polished cow bone. Today, you can find heavy acrylic versions.

Crop-A-Dile: A combination hole punch and eyelet setter, this craft tool is a must for every paper crafter. The tool is designed to punch through and set eyelets in everything from lightweight papers to cardboard, plastics, tin, and other metals.

Eyelets: Eyelets are small metal rings used to reinforce a hole in fabric or paper. They're available in a wide assortment of colors and sizes, making them a fun embellishment for invitations and programs. The heavy-duty version of an eyelet,

called a grommet, is used for projects that are made of thick materials or have holes larger than $3/8$ in. in diameter.

Cuttlebug: If there ever was a gift to the paper crafting world, the Cuttlebug is it. Primarily a die-cutting machine, the Cuttlebug uses sharp metal plates (dies) to punch shapes out of paper. You can also purchase textured plates and folders that allow you to dry emboss patterns onto paper projects. Yes, it can be pricey but trust me on this, you'll use your heavy-duty (and totally cute!) machine many, *many* times over for card-making and scrapbooking.

Paper punches: A vast array of paper punches is available in the wide world. From those that make simple holes to those that make more ornate designs, paper punches can be found in thousands of shapes and sizes to fit almost any style or motif.

Sewing equipment

All-purpose thread: I recommend a polyester or cotton-wrapped polyester thread for sewing most fabrics, whether by hand or on a machine.

Needles: For handsewn projects, keep a selection of needles in different sizes at the ready. Most needles are sold in large-quantity variety packs so you can do just that.

Pins: Use pins with plastic or glass heads. They're easy to see.

Sewing machine: Though there are small, inexpensive "craft" sewing machines on the market, you'll be better served by using a regular sewing machine. They're typically more reliable and sturdier than the cheap machines, and that'll save you a ton of frustration when it comes time for a scrapbooking or paper project involving sewing.

General

In addition to the specialty tools and gadgets just described, I recommend having all of the following tools on hand, most of which you're probably already familiar with:

- No. 2 pencils
- Cellophane tape
- Emery boards

- Craft knife blades
- Gum erasers
- Hammer
- Permanent markers
- Ruler and straightedge
- Sponge paintbrushes
- White pencil

Tried-&-True Techniques

If you're new to crafting, a few of the techniques mentioned in this book may seem a little intimidating. Don't worry! Most of the projects have been designed specifically for first-timers and novice crafters.

To help you navigate your way through a successful project, here is an introduction to the basic techniques used in this book.

Using a bone folder

1. Score the paper or card with the tip of the bone folder. This makes a line or depression in the paper so that it is easier to fold.

2. Fold the paper along the crease you made, and gently press flat.

3. Smooth the crease with the broad side of the bone folder using slight pressure. This will make a crisp fold in the paper.

Using a rubber stamp

1. Tap the rubber stamp surface onto an ink pad. Be gentle! It doesn't take a lot of pressure to ink a stamp. If you press too hard or rub the stamp along the surface of the ink pad, you'll get too much ink on your stamp and ruin your pads. Too much ink will bleed through your paper or smudge the image.

2. Hold the stamp firmly and press down on the paper or card. Do not rock or move the stamp. You'll smudge your image.

3. Lift the stamp straight up.

4. After you're done stamping, clean your stamp per the manufacturer's instructions.

Setting eyelets

1. Place paper onto a self-healing mat.

2. Use a small circle hole punch the size of your eyelet or the punch end of an eyelet-setting tool to make a hole in your paper.

3. If using a setting tool, hit the top of the tool with a hammer to punch a hole through the paper.

4. Place the eyelet into the hole so that the top side of the eyelet is on the front side of the paper.

5. Turn the paper over so that the top of the eyelet is facing down. Position the eyelet-setting tool over the eyelet and hit the end of the tool with a hammer. The back of the eyelet will spread out. Remove the eyelet tool and completely flatten the back of the eyelet with the hammer, if needed.

Using a wood burning tool

1. Read the manufacturer's instructions for the wood burning tool before plugging it in.

2. Allow the tool to heat up before attempting to use it. The hotter the tip, the easier it'll be to burn images into the wood or paper.

3. Place the hot wood tool tip gently on the surface to be burned. With smooth, even strokes press the tip firmly along the wood as you draw or trace your design. Don't leave the tool in one spot too long—you'll end up with extra-crispy spots on your project! The more times you pass over a line or design, the darker it'll get.

4. Always allow the tool to completely cool before you stow it away.

Using a Cuttlebug

1. Lower the platforms on both sides of the machine.

2. Place cutting material and die (face up) between the cutting pads or embossing folder.

3. Turn the handle to move the die or embossing folder through the machine.

4. Remove die-cut or embossed paper from the cutting pads or embossing folder.

Wedding Bliss Checklist

You've got a wedding to plan, a million details to attend to, plenty of projects to keep you busy, and a real life vying for top spot on your priority list. There's a lot on your plate, busy bee, and as the next few months whiz by, you want to be sure to make the most of them.

The surefire path to sanity during the wedding planning madness you're about to embark on is to get yourself organized. Right now, little missy (and mister)! To make that as easy as possible, look for the super-informative sidebar with the scissors icon (at right) that shows up at the start of each project. It'll let you know how much time to set aside and how many crafters you'll want on hand to help.

You'll also see a Crafty Calculator section in each project. This is a budgeting and cost comparison tool that is absolutely crucial for the prudent planner. You'll see what to budget and what kind of savings you can expect to enjoy by going the DIY Bride route.

Now that you know what to look for, I've put to-gether a nifty timeline that will take you from 12 months out all the way down to the last 6 hours before you walk down the aisle, and beyond. And at the end of timeline, look for the Project Planning Sheet that you can copy and personalize for each project, so that all the details you need are in one convenient place.

Time Wise
Here's where you'll find how long each project takes to complete. Use this as a general guideline, but the actual time it takes may vary because everyone's skill set and level of obsessive-compulsive behavior vary widely.

A Little Me Time
These are great solo projects for the bride-to-be.

Just the Two of Us
These projects are made for quality "us time" for you and your honey.

It's a Girl Thing
Sometimes you just need to ditch the guys to hang with your BFFs. Grab your girlfriends and have some fun while you complete these projects.

Divide & Conquer
Enlist the help of friends and family to make light work of these more labor-intensive projects. Do-it-yourself doesn't mean do it *all* by yourself!

12–9 Months to Go!

◯ All of your wedding details will be based on a few key decisions, so they need to be in place before you can move forward: the date and time of the wedding, the ceremony and reception locations, and the number of guests.

◯ Create a list of the projects you'd like to make for your wedding. Keep them in mind when thinking about your budget, schedule, and wedding theme.

◯ For each project, use the handy-dandy Project Planning Sheet on p. 19 so you can keep track of all the details—when you'll do the project, who is going to lend a hand, and the supplies you'll need, and where to get them.

◯ Start talking about a realistic budget with your sweetheart. Now's the time to begin saving your cash and comparison shopping for the best deals on supplies and services.

◯ Don't be caught off guard when gifts start rolling in right after you become engaged. Have a few From the Heart Thank-You Cards (p. 49) on hand so that you're always ready to send heartfelt thanks.

◯ Schedule a shoot with your photographer as soon as possible if you're using professional shots in any of your save-the-date mailings or invitations. Allow for plenty of time to get back proofs, order prints, and schedule any reshoots (not that you'll need them, gorgeous you!).

8–6 Months to Go!

◯ Think about the details you want to include in your wedding that will make it truly yours. What's your theme or color scheme? Start buying supplies that fit your style and vision.

◯ It's invitation planning time! The sooner you start your invitations, the better, as these usually take longer to complete than couples expect.

◯ Send out save-the-dates to your out-of-town guests.

◯ Take inventory of your time-commitments and obligations. Get a grip on how much free time you have to devote to all of the projects you want to complete, and talk to friends and family about helping out. This is the first step in preventing DIY overwhelm.

◯ This is the perfect time to check off the few smaller projects on your to-do list that you can handle on your own, like the Lace Flower-Girl's Basket (p. 77), Memorial Candle (p. 81), and Wire Bird's-Nest Ring Pillow (p. 85).

5–3 Months to Go!

○ Making a few projects that reflect your sense of style will really make the wedding yours. Check out the Bridal Headband (p. 91) and Ribbon & Lace Bridal Slipper (p. 103) for easy, customizable projects.

○ There's a bachelorette party in your future! Grab your maid of honor to discuss plans for your last hurrah as a single girl. Coordinate a date and time and show her that lovely Day Spa Bachelorette Party Invite on p. 111 for inspiration.

○ Buy supplies and create the Feather Boutonnieres (p. 107) for the groom and the guys in the wedding party.

○ Need another quickie project to check off of your seemingly endless to do list? The Embellished Bridal Wrap (p. 99) can be done in under 1 hour. Don't you just love it?

○ Don't forget about the maids! Make a pair of Bridesmaid Button Hairpins (p. 95) for each of them, according to your wedding theme or each gal's particular style.

8–4 Weeks to Go!

○ Time to think about the actual ceremony. Whether your event will be religious or secular, when you walk down the aisle or mingle with friends and family at the reception, you'll see the gorgeous results of all your hard work.

○ You deserve your name in lights—or at least your initials in glitter! Assemble the Glitter & Shine Monogram (p. 127). Be sure to check whether your venue allows you to use nails or pins to hang items on the doors or walls. If not, this project works well displayed on the cake table, the bride and groom's table, a mantel, or a windowsill.

○ A wedding program is a great memento for your guests at the ceremony. Design and create the Sew Divine Ceremony Program (p. 123), and remember to keep a few extras as keepsakes!

○ For full-on fondant fun, my retro brides, create the adorable Groovy Owl Cake Topper (p. 135).

○ Follow up with any vendors and venues about last-minute details: balances due, any changes to service, or updates for the guest list.

3–1 Week to Go!

◯ Your guest list is complete, your seating is finalized, and now it's time to schedule a handful of solo projects. Budget some alone time during these last few weeks to decompress while you polish off some crafty reception essentials.

◯ Once you've decided on your getaway car (or horse-drawn carriage, Vespa® scooter, or hot air balloon) create the Just-Married Banner (p. 159)!

◯ Think about all the friends and family who are coming together to celebrate your big day as you create the Magnetic Clothespin Seating Chart (p. 153).

◯ Sit back, put your feet up, and take some time to reminisce. Making the Memory Lane Table Marker (p. 145) will have you thinking about your amazing history before you embark on your blissfully married future.

◯ Wouldn't it be genius to keep the celebration going with a post-wedding brunch? This is a great way for those closest to you to bid you bon voyage before your honeymoon. Take a look at the Post-Wedding Brunch Place Setting (p. 163), a fashionable fix for morning-after festivities.

◯ Being a DIY Bride means putting your personal stamp on your wedding, so let's get literal with the stamped Cocktail Napkin (p. 149)! Your guests won't soon forget this detail.

6–2 Days to Go!

◯ You're so on track for your one-of a kind wedding. Keep up the crafty momentum in this final push. Show your guests how happy you are to have them at your wedding by carefully crafting the favor of your choice like the Cupcake in a Jar Favor (p. 169), or Milk & Cookies Favor (p. 175). Beseech a friend with an eye for design to organize the display of the party favors at the reception (it's just a few days away!). You'll have volunteers lining up once you bribe them with the delicious treats you've created.

◯ Make Customized Water Bottle Labels (p. 179) and have the bottles ready to go for thirsty celebrators at the reception.

◯ Don't let these hectic days get the best of you. Take a moment or two to relax with your sweetheart and remember what this whole thing is about.

1 Day to Go!

○ You're oh-so close! Relieve any logistics-related stress by indulging in some pre-wedding pampering so that you will be your glowing, gorgeous self tomorrow.

○ Coordinate the assembly, pick-up, and delivery of ceremony and reception projects with your helpers. Double-check that a few gentle hands will hang the Carnation Pomander (p. 189) on the chairs or pews. And ask a few Zen friends to work with the Asian Rock & Bamboo Centerpiece (p. 193).

○ Make sure your munchie-afflicted guests will be able get their hands on a treat tomorrow at the Gourmet Popcorn Buffet (p. 197).

○ Confirm any last-minute changes with your vendors, wedding party, and helpers.

6 Hours to Go!

○ Can you believe it? It's the Big Day! You've made it! You are hours away from walk-ing down the aisle, and that means finishing touches can be left in the capable hands of your most trusted pals:

○ A flock of early birds will assemble the Lily Bloom Bouquet (p. 203).
○ A tag-team will tackle the Flower & Citrus Centerpiece (p. 207).
○ Say "Cheese!" A tech-savvy pal will put up the DIY Photo Booth (p. 211).

Post-Wedding

○ Aaaaaaand exhale! You've got a nice tan, and there's a slice of cake stowed safely in the freezer. Now it's time to say thanks to everyone who made your one-of-a-kind wedding happen. Send thank-you notes for gifts received at or after the wedding.

○ Upcycle your ab fab Crafty Countdown wedding crafts, so you've got good vibes around at all times. The Magnetic Clothespin Seating Chart (p. 153) you made will keep your office organized—just clip important notes to it! The containers from the popcorn buffet make great container gardens, and use the light pro-jector from the Love in Lights Wall Projection (p. 119) to prep your next mural!

○ Take a look at the silly and sweet memories your friends and family captured in your DIY Photo Booth scrapbook.

Project Planning Sheet

Project Name: _____

Project Timing:
- ○ 12–9 months to go!
- ○ 8–6 months to go!
- ○ 5–3 months to go!
- ○ 8–4 weeks to go!
- ○ 3–1 week to go!
- ○ 6–2 days to go!
- ○ 1 day to go!
- ○ 6 hours to go!

Supplies Needed:	Helpers:	Phone/e-mail:	Assigned Task:

Does this require delivery and/or setup to the wedding venue?   ○ YES (details below)   ○ NO

Helper: _____   Phone/e-mail: _____   Date/Time: _____

Notes/Details: _____
_____
_____
_____

{Copy this sheet for each project.}

12

11

10

9

Months to go!

12-9 Months to Go!

ENGAGEMENT INVITES, SAVE-THE-DATES & THANK-YOUS

Even though your wedding seems so far away, there's plenty you can do right now to get started with your do-it-yourself celebration. The projects in this chapter are easy, entry-level stationery crafts that'll give you high-class results and get you geared up for your pre-wedding events. Kick off your crafty endeavors with engagement announcements. Your extended family and friends will love learning about your "off the market" status. Next, create and get out your save-the-dates to out-of-town guests. They'll need plenty of time to make travel plans. Finally, have thank-you notes on hand at all times. You'll be surprised by how frequently gifts and goodies are bestowed upon you throughout your wedding planning stages. Never let an opportunity to say thanks go by!

Important Dates

January 17 - Dress shopping at 10:00 a.m.

Dress Shopping
with the girls
1/17 - 10 Am

January 2009

S	M	T	W	T	F	S
				1	2	3
4	5	6	7	8	9	10
11	12	13	14	15	16	17
18	19	20	21	22	23	24
25	26	27	28	29	30	31

Pencil Me in Calendar

There's no denying that you have become extraordinarily adept at micromanaging every aspect of your wedding details. As soon as you said yes to your beloved's proposal, weird neurons started firing in the deep recesses of your brain and, quite suddenly, you became the most organized human being on the planet. Unfortunately, this wedding planning bug is not communicable, and your bridal party will remain as unorganized and forgetful as ever.

This project is designed to appeal to your innermost control-freak tendencies by creating a calendar of events to keep those maids and groomsmen in line and on schedule. Seriously, it's like herding cats sometimes.

Time Wise

Once your dates are plugged into the calendar, you can complete this project in 1 hour or so.

•

A Little Me Time

Your bridesmaids will be pitching in a lot in the coming months, so give them a break and tackle this crafty creation solo.

SUPPLIES

- Computer with Microsoft® Word
- Card stock, 4 in. by 9 in.
- Printer
- Stapler
- Patterned paper, cut into 4-in. by 2-in. strips
- Bone folder
- Double-sided tape, 1/4 in. wide
- Crop-A-Dile hole punch and eyelet setter tool
- Eyelets

These customized planners give you ample space to mark must-not-miss dates and add all the details your family and friends will need to be in the know—just like you. Think dress and tux fittings, bachelor parties and spa days, and, of course, the big day itself. And if you've got the space and the info is finalized, don't hesitate to include location addresses, phone numbers, websites, or directions. You can also scribble important notes and personalized messages in each of these fab booklets. They'll thank you for this . . . someday.

DIRECTIONS

1. The first step is to create the calendar sheets for the project in Microsoft Word. After opening a Word document, click on the Paper Size bar, scroll down, and select Manage Custom Sizes. On the bottom of the dialog box that appears, click the + button and enter "4 x 9" into the field. This creates a custom page size. In the fields on the right side of the dialog box, enter "4" for the height and "9" for the width. Use "0.25" for the top, bottom, left, and right margins. Click OK. This will drop you back to the Page Setup menu. Click the Portrait orientation, and then click OK again. You're done with this step. Congrats! It was the hardest part.

2. Next, you'll insert a calendar template onto the page. From the top of the page you just created, hit the return key until the cursor is about two-thirds of the way down the page.

3. From the Gallery toolbar, click Quick Tables. Scroll through the menu that appears to find the calendar template that best fits your style. Double-click it, and it will appear on the page. The Gallery toolbar and Quick Tables feature are available in newer versions of Microsoft Word. If your version of Word does not have these options, visit my website (www.diybride.com) and download calendar templates that will work whether you are on a PC or a Mac. Then you can copy and paste the template into your document.

4. To move the calendar template elsewhere on the page, click on the border of the calendar and drag it to wherever suits you. You can also adjust the calendar size by clicking on the lower-right corner and dragging the border with your mouse.

5. Customize your calendar by inserting the proper dates for each month you are including, changing the font type, color, and size as you wish. And do insert the name of the month somewhere on the page, so that you and your guests don't get confused about the dates you are looking at. Have fun with this step! Don't be afraid to play around with different fonts, borders, and graphics.

6. If you have dates that you don't want anyone to miss, go ahead and add them to the upper part of the calendar by creating a text box and inserting the event details. Leave at least a 1.5-in. margin at the top of your calendar page to allow for the eyelet and decorative paper topper.

7. I find it's easiest to create and save a separate page for each month leading up to the big day. It makes adjustments easier, and you needn't worry about altering the format of other pages when you make a simple change.

8. Print your calendar pages onto the 4-in. by 9-in. card stock and collate them into a neat stack for each person in your party. To secure the stack, staple the pages about ¼ in. from the top, in the center of the stack.

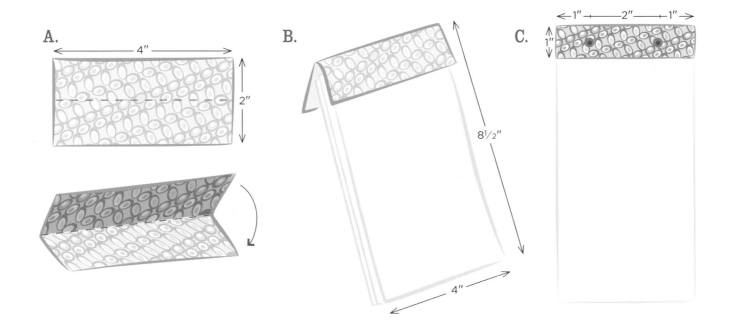

A.

4"

2"

B.

8½"

4"

C.

←1"→ ←2"→ ←1"→

1"

9. Now fold each strip of 4-in. by 2-in. patterned paper in half lengthwise (drawing A). Smooth out the crease with a bone folder. Add double-sided tape to the inside of the paper on the front and back flaps.

10. Fold the taped patterned paper over the top of one of the calendars, making sure the edges of the decorative paper and calendar pages are aligned and even (drawing B). Press down on the flaps to secure the tape to the paper.

11. Using the Crop-A-Dile tool, punch two holes in the top of the calendar stack, in the decorative paper border, about 1 in. in from each side and ½ in. from the top (drawing C). Now insert an eyelet into one of the holes and use the Crop-A-Dile tool to set the eyelet. Do the same for the other eyelet. That's all there is to it! If you'd like, add extra embellishment by threading ribbon through the eyelets.

tips & hints

- Remember, Microsoft Word is different for PCs and Macs, so if you're having problems, click on Help for assistance.

- The Crop-A-Dile tool has become one of my most indispensable craft tools. It costs about $20, but will last forever. If you're going to do any project that requires eyelets, brads, or punched holes, this is a must-have tool. See p. 10 for more details.

- This calendar can be made in any size you'd like. It looks fantastic as a square or printed as a full page. Just keep postage in mind if you are going to send the calendar through the mail.

- Adding a strip of magnetic tape to the back of the calendar is a savvy touch that'll allow your wedding party members to stick the calendar on their fridge as a handy reminder.

- Eyelets come in a rainbow of colors and styles. Hit up your local scrapbook stores for the best selection and most creative designs.

12

11

10

9

Months to go!

Crafty Calculator

WHAT TO BUDGET

Patterned paper	$0.60
Solid colored card stock (2 pages per calendar)	$0.20
Eyelets (2 per calendar)	$0.10
Total	$0.90

COST COMPARISON

I haven't seen these for sale on the bridal market yet. Custom calendars can be found at most online picture-printing services and prices vary widely from just a few dollars to well over $20.00 per piece. Crafty brides can make these at home for just $0.90.

STORE COST	YOUR COST
$20.00	**90¢**

Please join us for
An engagement celebration

Saturday, July 09
4.00 p.m.
5463 College Avenue

Please RSVP to Jennifer Leighton
At 458-8870
By June 20th

Katerina
&
Vincent

Picture Perfect
Engagement Party Invite

Congrats, you fabulous couple: You're engaged! Not only does this mean you will be joining your life with Your One True Love, but it also means that you now have an excuse to throw a once-in-a-lifetime fête. If we were pals and you lived close by, I'd totally host it for you. In lieu of that, I'm handing you a great engagement party invite that's modern and elegant with a little bit of flair.

This is an easy project for crafters-in-training and seasoned pros alike. I highly recommend grabbing a few handy-with-scissors friends to help with cutting the photographs for the invite into the curvy bracket shape. Great company, music, and food will make everything seem less like a chore and more like a party!

Time Wise

Assembling the invites is super easy. Once you've chosen your photo and created your Microsoft Word document, you can create about 10 completed invitations in 30 minutes.

It's a Girl Thing

Brew up your best batch of espresso and invite your girlfriends over for a high-octane crafting session (it can't hurt to throw some chocolate in the mix to add to the caffeine buzz)!

SUPPLIES

- Picture Perfect Engagement Party Invite Template copied onto card stock or paper (below)
- Photo of you and your wonderful fiancé
- Pencil with eraser
- Scissors
- Computer with Microsoft Word
- Color printer
- Card stock, cut to 4 in. by 9 in.
- Double-sided tape

STATION 1: TRACING
This is an easy task for your maids because tracing the template onto the photo is simple.

STATION 2: PRINTING
If you haven't printed your invites in advance, man the printer and oversee the group's progress.

STATION 3: CUTTING
Put your girls with an eye for detail at the cutting station. A perfect cut makes your invitations look professionally done.

STATION 4: FINAL ASSEMBLY
This group brings it all together. Have them address and stuff the envelopes, and affix the postage.

DIRECTIONS

1. The easiest way to start this project is to create the curvy pictures of you and your fiancé. To do this, copy the photograph template (below) onto a piece of card stock or paper. Cut the template shape out. Place the template on the printed photo and trace around it with a pencil onto each photo. Cut the photo along the lines you've just traced and set it aside. Repeat this for all the photos.

2. Next, create your invitation in Microsoft Word. Go to File and choose Page Setup. From the Paper Size bar, scroll down and select Manage Custom Sizes. On the bottom of the dialog box that appears, click the + button and enter "4 x 9" into this field. This creates a custom page size. In the fields to the right side of the dialog box, enter "4" for the height and "9" for the width. Use "0.25" for the top, bottom, left, and right margins. Click OK. This will drop you back to the Page Setup menu. Click the Landscape orientation, and then click OK again. You now have a template for your 4-in. by 9-in. invitation.

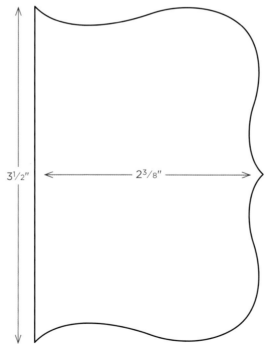

$3^1/_2$" $2^3/_8$"

Picture Perfect Engagement Party Invite Template

Trace or reproduce this template for your invitation.

3. Since you'll be adding your bracket-shaped photo to the left of the invitation, you'll want to print the invitation wording only on the right side. To do this, create a text box on the right-hand side of the template. You can adjust the size any time by clicking on one corner of the text box and dragging it with your mouse.

4. Click inside the text box and insert your invitation wording. Save your document and then print it on the 4-in. by 9-in. card stock.

5. You're almost done! Once your invitations are printed, the last step is to affix the photos to the invitation. For each one, flip a photo over and place double-sided tape on the back. Turn it over and line up the straight edges of the invitation and photo, so when you press the photo in place, the edges will be flush. Center the photo so that you have approximately $1/2$ in. of card stock above and below the photo. Press the photo onto the invitation firmly to get a solid bond.

tips & hints

- Remember, Microsoft Word is different for PCs and Macs, so if you're having problems, click on Help for assistance.

- The best photo size for the photo template is 4 in. tall by about 3½ in. wide. Don't be afraid to play around with different sizes, though!

- While you can use actual photo prints, an easier and cheaper method is to scan your photo and print it on photo-quality paper directly from your printer.

- This invitation requires a business size envelope. These can be found in dozens of colors and with different styles of flaps and openings. Check out your local stationery stores for unique envelope designs.

- Want to add a little something extra to the cards? Use clip art, monograms, rubber stamps, ribbon, or crystals to embellish your invitation.

Crafty Calculator

WHAT TO BUDGET

Card stock (per sheet)	$0.10
Photo printing	$0.10
Cost per invite	$0.20

COST COMPARISON

Custom-designed photo invitations will cost about $2.00 each from stationers. This do-it-yourself invitation will set you back only $0.20.

STORE COST	YOUR COST
$2.00	**20¢**

Please Save The Date
October 10, 2010
For Tina & Mark's Wedding
In The Beautiful Forests Of
Yosemite National Park
Details To Follow

S'mores Save-the-Date Kit

Every year a group of my girlfriends and I get together for an all-girl camping weekend. We commune with nature, ditch our guys, catch up on each others' lives, and gorge ourselves on amazing campground goodies. (Whoever said camping is "roughing it" has never been to one of our events!)

On my year as camp organizer, I made a save-the-date that's still talked about years later: the s'mores save-the-date. Filled with handmade marshmallows, gourmet graham crackers, and exotic chocolates, the save-the-date package was a smash with my girly group of foodies.

If you're planning a beach, mountain, or other outdoorsy wedding location, this is a fun (and delicious!) way to alert your guests of your upcoming nuptials. The great thing about this project is that you needn't go upscale with it if you don't want to.

Time Wise

Once you've designed and printed out your labels, you can expect to create four to six save-the-dates in 1 hour.

Just the Two of Us

This is a fun project to do with your sweetie in front of a roaring fire (or improvise with some romantic candles!). If you can trust your hubby-to-be not to eat all the treats, assign him the task of filling the bags. But if his sweet tooth has the tendency to run rampant, have him cut the save-the-date labels from the card stock sheets.

SUPPLIES

- Computer with Microsoft Word
- Printer
- Card stock for the labels, cut to 2½ in. by 2½ in.
- Paper cutter or scissors
- Bone folder
- Card stock, cut to 4 in. by 3 in.
- Graham cracker squares
- Marshmallows
- Chocolate squares
- Clear treat bag, 3 in. wide by 4 in. tall
- Stapler
- Ribbon, 10 in. long
- Double-sided tape

Store-brand graham crackers, marshmallows, and regular chocolate bars work just as well and are a heck of a lot cheaper when you're buying them in bulk.

These are best when hand-delivered to your nearby guests or when they're sent in cool weather months. Chocolate tends to melt during shipping so, please, keep that in mind when you send your yummy mailings.

DIRECTIONS

1. Let's kick off the project with the hardest part first: creating the printed save-the-date label. Open Microsoft Word and create a new 8.5-in. by 11-in. document.

2. Create a text box that's 2½ in. by 2½ in. To do this, click the Text Box icon on the Drawing Toolbar. Click onto the blank document and drag your cursor to create a box. To adjust the size of the box, double click on it and a dialog box will pop up in which you'll be able to input the exact size you need. Just click on the Size tab and type in "2.5 x 2.5."

3. Insert the text—or a piece of clip art—into the text box. Make sure the typeface is easy to read—it will be smaller once it's printed out on the save-the-date card—and keep the information as simple as possible. Guests need to know the big three: *who* is getting married, *where* the shindig is, and *when* they should mark their calendars.

4. Once you have a design you love, select the text box by double-clicking it. Copy and paste the box multiple times in the document, leaving space between each copy. The idea is to fit as many copies as you can on one sheet without overlapping the design. Save the document and print it on the card stock for the labels.

5. Finally, cut the save-the-date labels from the card stock sheets with scissors or a paper cutter.

6. Time to create the bag topper! With a bone folder, score and crease the 4-in. by 3-in. piece of card stock in half, so each half measures 2 in. by 3 in. This is the part of the project when you can do nearly anything you want. You can use beautifully patterned paper, add a line of romantic poetry in calligraphy, or decorate the card stock with rubber stamps— don't be afraid to play with this area of real estate.

7. Now, the fun part: filling the treat bags with goodies! Insert two graham crackers, 1 chocolate piece, and 1 marshmallow into each bag. Fold the top of the bag down a couple of times and staple the fold to keep it closed.

8. Wrap a piece of ribbon lengthwise around the entire bag of s'mores, and secure it at the top of the bag with double-sided tape (drawing A).

A.

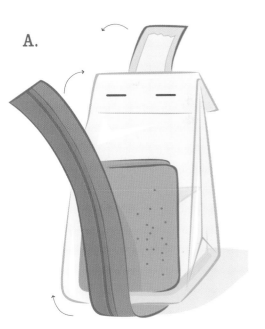

12
11
10
9

Months to go!

B.

9. Apply double-sided tape on the inside flaps of the topper. Affix the topper to the top of the bag, over the stapled fold (drawing B).

10. Last of all, add the label to the front. Apply double-sided tape to the back of the label and center it on the front of the save-the-date.

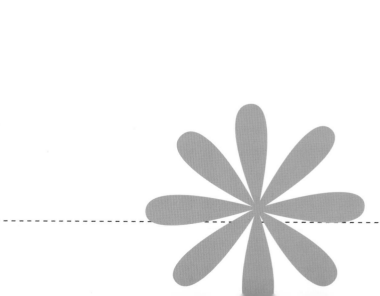

tips & hints

- Remember, Microsoft Word is different for PCs and Macs, so if you're having problems, click on Help for assistance.

- Buy plenty of extra graham crackers for this project. I found that each box I bought had at least a few broken crackers that couldn't be used.

- Make this project upscale by using exotic chocolates, hand-crafted marshmallows, and gourmet graham crackers.

- Conversely, you can go super cheap on this project by using regular store-brand goodies—an equally yummy treat.

- These save-the-dates are perishable, so pay your nearby guests a visit and deliver the goods in person. If you're sending them via the postal service, use a sturdy box and plenty of padding to help prevent breakage.

Warning: If sending during warm weather months, the chocolates will *melt.*

Crafty Calculator

WHAT TO BUDGET

Chocolates	$0.20
Marshmallows	$0.05
Graham crackers	$0.05
Bags	$0.15
Ribbon	$0.20
Card stock (per sheet)	$0.10
Total per save-the-date	$0.75

COST COMPARISON

I've not yet seen anything like this on the wedding market. For comparison, gourmet s'mores can cost $3.00 each at upscale confectioners. Add on a simple save-the-date and you're looking at $4.00 or more for something similar. Ours costs $0.75 each using supplies that are easy to find in our local grocery and craft supply stores.

STORE COST	YOUR COST
$4.00	75¢

12
11
10
9

Months to go!

SAVE THE DATE !

Amy Elizabeth
and
Ricky James

are getting married
on Saturday, December
10th, 2011
in Honolulu, Hawaii

Details to follow soon.

Aloha Save-the-Date & Envelope

For many couples, sending out save-the-dates is a chore with rigid rules and little imagination. "Dear friends and family, we're getting married next year. Here are the dates. Details to come." Yawn! You're so *not* that couple. You have personality, for goodness sake, and a deep appreciation for kitsch. Your family and friends have come to terms with your tiki fixation and obsession with lowbrow art. In fact, they actually expect something fun and different from your wedding experience. This save-the-date will not disappoint.

Paying homage to vintage Hawaiiana, this tropical beauty is a nifty way to get your guests guessing about the luau-o-rama wedding fest

Time Wise

Once your invitation has been printed, you can assemble about four invitations in 1 hour.

Divide & Conquer

To help speed things along, get a few friends together to lend a hand with stamping, cutting, and creating the envelopes while sipping tropical mocktails and listening to your favorite Hawaiian beach tunes.

SUPPLIES

- 2 sheets of white card stock, $8\frac{1}{2}$ in. by 11 in.
- 1 roll of grass cloth wallpaper
- Craft knife
- Bone folder
- Red line double-sided tape
- Computer with Microsoft Word
- Printer
- White card stock, $4\frac{1}{4}$ in. by $5\frac{1}{2}$ in.
- Red card stock, $4\frac{1}{2}$ in. by $5\frac{3}{4}$ in.
- Flower and leaf (or other) tropical-themed rubber stamps
- Dye-based rubber stamp inks in red and green
- Glue stick
- Adhesive address and return address labels

STATION 1: ENVELOPES
Have one or two friends on hand to create the cool envelopes.

STATION 2: DOUBLE-STICKING
This group mounts the white card stock to the red card stock with double-sided tape.

STATION 3:
STAMPING, CUTTING, & GLUING
Let everyone stamp, but assign one friend with a steady hand to cut out your tiki blossoms; the others can glue the flowers to the save-the-dates.

STATION 4: FINAL ASSEMBLY
This group puts the save-the-dates into the envelopes, seals them, and applies the address labels and stamps.

---

that's in store for them. While it's a bit labor intensive, the result is a unique save-the-date that's so totally you.

What I love most about this project is the use of grass cloth wallpaper to create custom envelopes. It's an unexpected detail and something that you can pretty much be guaranteed no one else is doing.

DIRECTIONS

1. Let's start by getting those uber-cool custom-made envelopes out of the way. On a piece of $8\frac{1}{2}$-in. by 11-in. white card stock, draw your own envelope template according to the measurements in drawing A (at right). Now trace the template onto the back of the wallpaper.

2. Cut the envelopes from the wallpaper using a craft knife (or paper cutter). Score and fold the envelopes with a bone folder according to the dotted guidelines in drawing A.

3. Fold in the envelope's left and right flaps toward the center. Then fold up the bottom flap and adhere it to the side flaps with red line double-sided tape (see p. 8). Set the finished envelopes aside and move on to creating the save-the-dates.

4. Open Microsoft Word and create a new document. Create a custom page size by going to the File menu and clicking on Page Setup. From the Paper Size bar, scroll down and select Manage Custom Sizes. On the bottom of the dialog box that appears, click the + button and enter "4.25 x 5.5" into this field. This creates a custom page size. In the fields on the right side of the dialog box, enter "5.5" for the height and "4.25" for the width. Use "0.25" for the top, bottom, left, and right margins. Click OK. This will bring you back to the Page Setup menu. Click the Portrait orientation and then click OK again.

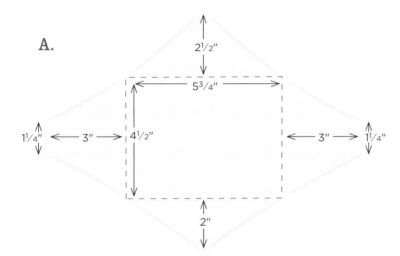

A.

2¹/₂"

5³/₄"

1¹/₄"   3"   4¹/₂"   3"   1¹/₄"

2"

B.

5. Enter your save-the-date information, grouping the text in the center of the page. Save your document and print the save-the-date onto the 4¹/₄-in. by 5¹/₂-in. white card stock.

6. Apply red line double-sided tape to the cards you just made and mount them onto the pieces of 4¹/₂-in. by 5³/₄-in. red card stock, being careful to center them so that there is an even ¹/₄-in. border on all four sides of the save-the-date.

7. Next up: rubber stamping! The first step is stamping a piece of white card stock with your flower stamp (or other tropical-themed stamp) using the red ink. Do this on a piece of white card stock—not directly onto the save-the-date. Let the ink dry, and then cut out the stamped flowers with a craft knife (drawing B). Set the cut-outs aside. Haven't used a rubber stamp before? No problem! Just read the tips on p. 12 and try stamping a few flowers on scrap paper until you get the hang of it.

8. Now that you're in the stamping groove, ink the leaf stamp with your green ink and press it directly onto the save-the-date near the top of the invitation, on the left-hand side (see photo on p. 38 for placement). Re-ink the stamp and add another leaf to the bottom right corner of the invitation to add visual balance. Let the ink dry completely.

9. Lastly, apply glue to the back of the cut-out flowers and adhere them to the save-the-date, slightly overlapping the leaf stamp at the top of the card. This adds a nice three-dimensional effect. Once the glue is dry, it's time to put the save-the-dates into the grass cloth wallpaper envelopes. Seal them shut with red line double-sided tape and apply an adhesive address label, a return address label, and a postage stamp to the front.

tips & hints

- Remember, Microsoft Word is different for PCs and Macs, so if you're having problems, click on Help for assistance.

- The world of rubber stamping is pretty vast. If tropical kitsch isn't your bag, there are thousands of designs available on the market to suit your fancy.

- Inks and ink pads come in a rainbow of colors to fit your color scheme. Don't be shy about mixing it up with unusual or unexpected color choices.

- Be careful when working with the grass cloth wallpaper. The grass can be brittle and will sometimes splinter when it's bent into the envelope shape. Getting poked is no fun, so trim off any splinters.

- One roll of wallpaper will yield over 100 envelopes. It's likely you'll have leftover paper. Don't let it go to waste! The leftovers can be used to make nifty tropical-inspired program covers, favor boxes, pew cones, or table runners.

- Many post offices will accept the envelopes; however, not every one will. Some offices are pickier than others. It's best to take a test save-the-date and envelope to your local post office and ask the clerk if he or she will accept it. If not, just slip the crafty invite and envelope into a mailer. The large outer envelopes can be found in great colors to coordinate with your invite. Check out the Resources (p. 214) for recommended paper goods sources.

Crafty Calculator

WHAT TO BUDGET

Card stock	$12.00
Wallpaper	$30.00
Rubber stamps	$12.00
Inks	$12.00
Total (for 50 save-the-dates)	$66.00

COST COMPARISON

Stationers charge around $150.00 or more for 50 custom save-the-date and envelope ensembles. Your tiki-licious DIY version will only cost $66.00 for 50 (only $1.32 each!) when made in bulk. And you'll have leftover supplies to use elsewhere in your wedding, which can cut your costs even more.

STORE COST	YOUR COST
$150.00	**$66.00**

Stuck on You
Save-the-Date

While you know—to the exact nanosecond—how far away your wedding day is, some of your guests will completely forget about it unless they have a constant reminder. Because you really can't tattoo your wedding date on your forgetful friends, and a cattle-prodding regimen is quite impractical, your "Hey! Remember my wedding date!" options are somewhat limited.

Might I suggest a fridge magnet? It's easy to make, recipient-friendly, and can be prominently displayed where the guest will see it every day. This handy little reminder will take only a few minutes to create and can be customized with any text or graphics you'd like. Bonus: It's pain free.

Time Wise

Depending on your skill level, you can expect to create anywhere from 2 to 6 completed save-the-dates in 1 hour.

Divide & Conquer

Many hands make light work. Gather your best buds and fave family members together for a light lunch and some heavy crafting.

SUPPLIES

- Bone folder
- Card stock, cut to 10 in. by 5 in.
- Computer with Microsoft Word
- Printer
- Printable magnet sheets, 8½ in. by 11 in., available at craft and office supply stores
- Scissors or paper cutter
- Patterned paper, 4 in. by 4 in.
- Double-sided tape

STATION 1: SCORING
This is an easy task for your helpers because scoring card stock is pretty simple.

STATION 2: MEASURING AND TAPING
Unless you totally trust your pals' hand–eye coordination, have this group measure, mark, and tape the patterned paper to the card stock.

STATION 3: CUTTING
Have this group cut out the magnets.

STATION 4: FINAL ASSEMBLY
This group brings it all together. Have the team affix the magnet to the patterned paper and then to the folded card stock.

DIRECTIONS

1. With a bone folder, score a line along the center of each 10-in. by 5-in. piece of card stock, dividing it into two 5-in. by 5-in. sections. Fold the card stock in half along the score mark and use the side of the bone folder to smooth down the fold. This creates a sharp, crisp crease in the card stock. You'll be attaching your save-the-date magnet to the front of the card and will be able to write a personal handwritten note to your guests on the inside. It's up to you whether you want the card to fold open like a book or flip up like a calendar, but be consistent so that the note inside corresponds with the orientation of the magnet on the front of the card!

2. Next, make the magnet labels in Microsoft Word. Create a new 8.5-in. by 11-in. document. Make a text box, 3 in. by 3 in. in size. To do this, click the Text Box icon on the Drawing toolbar. Click onto the blank document and drag your cursor to create a box. To adjust the size of the box, double-click it and a dialog box will pop up in which you'll be able to input the exact size you need. In this case, type in "3 x 3" after clicking the Size tab. Before you close this window, take a second to add a little pizzazz to your text box. Select the Colors and Lines tab and choose line colors and styles that correspond to your wedding scheme. Have fun playing around with this!

3. Insert the text—or a piece of clip art—into the text box. Make sure the font size and style are legible (the type will be smaller once it's printed out on the card) and don't overload the box with info. Simplicity and brevity are best.

4. Once you have a design you love, copy and paste the text box multiple times in the document, leaving a bit of space between each copy. The idea is to fit as many copies as you can on each sheet without overlapping the design. Save the document and print it on the magnet sheets.

5. Cut the 3-in.-square magnets from the sheets with scissors or a paper cutter. To complete the save-the-date magnets, affix a magnet (drawing A) to the

A.

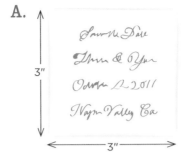

3"

3"

B.

4"

4"

C.

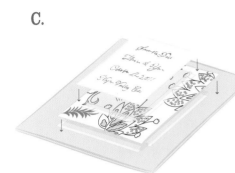

center of the 4-in. by 4-in. piece of patterned paper (drawing B) with double-sided tape.

6. With double-sided tape, center the magnet with its swanky, patterned paper border on the front of the 5-in. by 5-in. card you created in Step 1 (drawing C). Add your notes inside, and your magnetic save-the-dates are ready to grace the fridges of friends and family!

tips & hints

- *Remember, Microsoft Word is different for PCs and Macs, so if you're having problems, click on Help for assistance.*

- *This card can be scaled to any size you like. Envelopes for 5-in. by 5-in. cards are easy to find, and it's a fun size to work with. Other common square sizes are 4 in., 6 in., and 7 in., but try any shape you'd like. Keep in mind*

the U.S. Postal Service charges extra postage for square cards.

- *The inside of this card is left blank to accommodate a handwritten note to your guest. Do let them know that there is a magnet on the card. Add a little line such as, "As a reminder that our date is on the calendar, here's a small magnet for your refrigerator or office bulletin board."*

Crafty Calculator

WHAT TO BUDGET

Magnet sheet (12 save-the-dates per sheet)	**$7.00**
White card stock	**$0.20**
Patterned paper (6 cards per sheet)	**$0.70**
Total per save-the-date	**$0.90**

COST COMPARISON

Custom save-the-date magnets cost around $2.00 each. Crafty DIYers can make these at home—including the card—for about $0.90 each.

STORE COST	YOUR COST
$2.00	**90¢**

From the Heart
Thank-You Card

Face it, writing thank-you notes ranks pretty low on the fun scale. No matter how cool or wonderful the gift is, coming up with dozens of unique and clever ways to express your gratitude is mind-numbingly tedious. My own husband, bored out of his skull on one of our thank-you card nights, decided to amuse himself by thanking each of the gift-givers on his list by writing a little note about how wonderful their gift would be when we made tacos. While "Thank-you for the Cuisinart®. It'll be handy on taco night," works well for kitchen appliances, it was a complete non sequitur for things like sheets and towels. Don't let this happen to you!

Time Wise

Expect to complete 6 to 12 thank-you notes in 1 hour.

•

It's a Girl Thing

Although you probably can do this on your own, why not invite a few crafty girlfriends over to make the task a little easier? And speaking of taco night, show your thanks for their help by serving up some fresh guacamole, nachos, and margaritas. Who doesn't love that spread?

SUPPLIES

- From the Heart Thank-You Card Template (below)
- Pencil
- Scrap card stock, for template
- Pink card stock, 8½ in. by 11 in.
- Scissors
- Double-sided tape
- White card stock, cut to 7¼ in. by 3¼ in.
- Patterned paper, cut to 7¾ in. by 3¾ in.
- Bone folder
- Envelopes, 5 in. square

While I can't entirely save you from thank-you boredom, I can give you a whimsical thank-you card on which to write your most creative communiqués. This heart-shaped thank-you is a great little way to show your appreciation with style and, just maybe, make your thank-you nights a little brighter.

DIRECTIONS

1. Are you ready for a super-easy 5-minute project? Let's go! Copy the heart template below onto a piece of scrap card stock and then cut it out.
   If you have helpers, create a template for each person. It'll speed up the process.

From the Heart Thank-You Card Template

Trace or reproduce this template for your thank you card.

*Template shown at 50%. Enlarge to 200% for a full-size template.

STATION 1: TRACING
Have a few ladies tackle tracing the heart template onto pink card stock.

STATION 2: CUTTING
Put your girls with the steadiest hands on this task. A perfect cut makes your thank-you notes look professionally done.

STATION 3: FINAL ASSEMBLY
This group brings it all together. Unfortunately, the task of *writing* the notes lies with you, dear bride!

2. Trace the template onto the pink card stock and cut it out.

3. Next, add the inner layers of the thank-you note. Place strips of double-sided tape on the back of the white card stock and stick it to the front of the patterned paper, so the patterned paper makes an even border on all sides of the

A.

B.

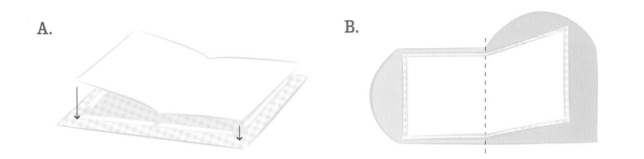

white card (drawing A). Now place double-sided tape on the back of the patterned paper and affix it to the inside of the pink heart, about ¼ in. from the straight, bottom edge (drawing B).

4. With a bone folder, create a crease down the center of the card (see dotted reference line on drawing B) and fold it over.

5. Now, write your most gracious thank-yous with beautiful ink on the inside of the card. Place the card into an envelope and—violà!—you're done.

tips & hints

- *Be aware about the postage for this card. The U.S. Postal Service charges extra postage for square cards.*

- *Any colors and patterns can be used for the paper in this project. Do try to choose a light color or faint pattern for the layer you'll write on so that your ink will show up.*

- *Handwritten notes are much more personal than those printed on a computer. But if your handwriting looks like hieroglyphics, don't be shy about using a computer to write your notes—just remember to sign them by hand.*

- *Use rubber stamps, paint pens, rhinestones, glitter, or other embellishments to make your note stand out.*

Crafty Calculator

WHAT TO BUDGET

Pink card stock (per sheet)	$0.10
Patterned paper (per sheet)	$0.10
White card stock (per sheet)	$0.05
Total per card	$0.25

COST COMPARISON

Die-cut cards can be quite expensive from stationery stores. Expect to pay anywhere from $2.50 to $6.00 for a single card. This adorable DIY card will cost you just $0.25.

STORE COST	YOUR COST
$6.00	**25¢**

8

7

6

Months to go!

8-6 Months to Go!

INVITATIONS & KEEPSAKES

Now that you're getting into a wedding planning routine, it's time to start a few of the more involved Big Day projects. Of course you'll want to get those invitations done. They'll need to be sent in just a few weeks, especially if you have overseas guests (airmail can take ages!). And for a break from papercrafts, try your hand at creating the Memorial Candle to honor someone special. It's a meaningful project and takes just minutes to complete. The Lace Flower-Girl's Basket is another quick, unique creation that can suit any wedding theme, not to mention any adorable little girl. There's something so utterly satisfying about ticking off projects from your to-do list, especially when you haven't had to toil or endure tedium to see a fabulous finished product.

Wood Laminate Invitation

While I don't dare declare paper as passé, I do predict that using unusual materials in invitations will continue to be a force in the wedding world for many years to come. As organic materials and inspired design continue to intersect, it's only natural that hip couples find ways to incorporate eco-friendly projects into their ultra-stylish events. This project is dedicated to all of my fellow tree-hugging, organic-loving, design snob friends.

For this invitation, wood veneer was an irresistible choice. Lightweight, flexible, and easy to print on, it's a clever substitution for plain old card stock. The embellishment of choice is a graphic design that's burned into the surface of the invitation with an inexpensive wood burning tool found at most craft and hobby stores.

Time Wise

Preparing and printing the invitation will go fairly quickly, but using the wood burning tool takes extra care and time to get clean lines. Allow yourself at least 10 to 15 minutes per invitation.

Just the Two of Us

Some men are "allergic" to crafting. You may ask your honey for help with the invites, and he'll head for the hills, but trust me on this: Burning wood + tools = fun for the fiancé. He'll dig this project big time.

SUPPLIES

- Rotary paper cutter or sharp craft knife
- Ruler
- Light-colored wood veneer like birch, unbacked, cut to 6 in. by 6 in.
- Computer with Microsoft Word
- Clip art
- Printer
- Wood burning tool with fine tip

The project is an easy one for beginners, but using the wood burning tool can take some practice. It's best to have pieces of scrap veneer around for trial runs so that you can get a feel for the tool.

DIRECTIONS

1. Using a heavy-duty rotary paper cutter or a sharp craft knife and ruler, cut the sheets of wood veneer (they usually come in 3-ft. sheets) into 6-in.-square pieces and set them aside.

2. Now create your invitation in Microsoft Word . Go to File and choose Page Setup. From the Paper Size bar, scroll down and select Manage Custom Sizes. On the bottom of the dialog box that appears, click the + button and enter "6 x 6" into the field. This creates a custom page size. In the fields on the right side of the dialog box, enter "6" for the height and width. Use "0.25" for the top, bottom, left, and right margins. Click OK. This will bring you back to the Page Setup menu. Click the Portrait orientation, and then click OK again. You've just created the template for your 6-in. by 6-in. invitation. Pat yourself on the back!

3. Now it's time to insert your invitation wording and clip art into the template. If you're a font junkie like me, you'll probably spend hours playing with this part of the invitation. That's okay!

4. Once you've found the perfect combination of fonts, clip art, layout, and wording save your document and prepare to print your invites. You'll notice that your veneer will have a grain to it, meaning that the piece will bend fairly easily along one axis, but will remain stiff if bent along the other. Orient all of your veneer pieces so that the "bendy" direction is parallel to the paper feed direction of your printer's roller. The veneer needs to conform to the roller as it prints. Otherwise the veneer may split or break inside your printer.

5. The next step is to print the invitation onto the wood veneer. For most printers, you'll have to feed each piece of veneer through by hand. Keep your sweetie on hand to help pass the time.

6. Plug in your wood burning tool, and let it heat up according to the manufacturer's instructions. Once the tool is heated and ready to go, it's time to get burning! Do this step in a well-ventilated space. Smoke from the burning wood can be irritating. With a light, slow touch, press the hot tip of the tool to the surface of your wood invitation, using the clip art or wording as a tracing guide (drawing A). It may take more than one pass to get a dark, even burn. Have a few extra pieces of veneer on hand in case you want to get a feel for the tool.

A.

tips & hints

- *Remember, Microsoft Word is different for PCs and Macs, so if you're having problems, click on Help for assistance.*

- *Many veneer companies offer sample packs of their veneers. These are great to get an idea of the types, colors, and thicknesses of the veneers that are out there. You'll also be able to verify that your printer can accept veneer through its feeder.*

- *For the best print quality, make sure the clip art you use is at least 150 dpi.*

- *Many wood burning tools come with multiple tips. Don't be afraid to experiment with different ones to create your own unique design.*

- *If the edges of your invitations are rough, a nail file or emery board is perfect for sanding away imperfections.*

- *Use rubber stamps, paint pens, rhinestones, glitter, or other embellishments to make sure your invite gets noticed.*

Crafty Calculator

WHAT TO BUDGET

Wood burning tool	$20.00
Veneer sheet	$25.00
Envelopes (50 pack)	$ 9.50
Total (for 50 invites)	$54.50

COST COMPARISON

Custom veneer invitations can cost upward of $1,250.00 for 50 invitation sets (invitation, response card, and envelopes). Our do-it-yourself version costs just $54.50 for 50 invites and envelopes.

STORE COST	YOUR COST
$1,250.00	**$54.50**

Destination Wedding Map Guide

Being engaged is supposed to be a time of bliss and utter happiness, right? So, why are you dreaming of running away to lush, exotic locales on your wedding day? Maybe it's the stress of planning a reception for 200 people (40 of them being members of your mom's Bunco® group whom you've never met), or maybe the lure of celebrating your new life in a tropical paradise seems more fitting than a rental hall in your hometown? Whatever your reasons for taking your wedding abroad, it's safe to say that doing it with panache is a top priority. Your ultra-stylish invitation should reflect that to set the mood for the adventure awaiting your guests.

Time Wise

After creating the templates and printing the guidebook pages, you can assemble about 5 invites in 1 hour.

Divide & Conquer

This is a project that calls for a few extra hands for cutting paper and assembling the booklets. Invite some friends over and have a cut-and-paste party! Be sure to have plenty of pairs of scissors on hand along with lots and lots of adhesive.

SUPPLIES

- Map of your destination location
- Tan card stock, 8½ in. by 11 in.
- Printer
- Chipboard album, luggage tag-shaped, about 3 in. by 5 in. when closed
- Spray adhesive
- Craft knife
- White copy paper, for template
- Pencil
- Black pen
- Scanner
- Computer with Microsoft Word
- White card stock or printer paper, 8½ in. by 11 in.
- Paper cutter or scissors
- Glue stick
- Circle punch, 1¼ in.
- Card stock
- Plastic compass
- Crop-A-Dile tool
- Twine, about 6 in.

STATION 1:
TRACING, GLUING & CUTTING
Have friends trace the album onto the tan card stock, spray the adhesive, and cut out the booklets. Remember to do this in a well-ventilated space!

STATION 2: PASTING PAGES
While you take on the tricky job of tracing, scanning, and creating the interior pages, let friends glue the printed pages into the booklet.

STATION 3: FINAL ASSEMBLY
This group adds the paper circle, compass, and twine.

As a travel enthusiast, I wanted to create something fun that fit the travel aspect of a destination wedding while offering guests all the essential information they need to get to there. This invitation takes a premade chipboard book, found at craft and scrapbooking stores, and turns it into a super-cool invitation and itinerary for the wedding ahead.

DIRECTIONS

1. The first step is to cover the outside of the chipboard album (found in craft and scrapbooking stores) with a color photocopy of a map of the wedding location. From your home copier or at a copy shop, photocopy your map onto a piece of tan card stock. If your map is already digitized and on your computer, simply print it onto card stock using your printer. Once your copies are made, open the chipboard album and lay it flat on the back of the printed card stock corresponding to the area of the map that you want to cover the front and back of your invite with. Trace the outline of the booklet onto the card stock with a pencil or a black pen. When tracing, add about ¼ in. to the short ends of the booklet to account for creases and bulges in the binding, so when it is time to fold the booklet, the map is a perfect fit.

2. In a well-ventilated space, apply spray adhesive inside the traced outline you just made on the back of the card stock (drawing A). Place the booklet on top of the outline and press it firmly in place with your fingers. Once the adhesive has dried per the manufacturer's recommended time, carefully cut closely

A.

along all the sides of the booklet with the craft knife. You now have your map-covered booklet!

3. The trickiest part of this project, creating the interior pages for the booklet, is next. (I know, the booklet already has pages inside, but we're creating custom-made pages so you can write all your crucial invite info and then paste the pages onto the existing ones in the booklet.) While it may take some time to get everything right, don't freak out! Once you nail the basic layout, the rest falls into place. Start by tracing the outline of the closed booklet onto a piece of plain white copy paper with a black pen. Do this twice, one outline underneath the other, and both oriented the same way. This will be scanned and saved onto your computer and used as the basis of the template in Microsoft Word. The traced images need to be straight and centered on the page. Be extra careful to avoid making any stray marks on the page. Make sure the outline is clean (no smudges!) and as dark as possible, so it'll show up well as a scanned image.

4. Scan the page onto your hard drive.

5. Open Microsoft Word. Create a new document. From the Page Layout or Format tab, select the Page Layout option, then the Watermark option. Click the Select Picture button and then find the scanned image you just created. Select it. Uncheck the Washout option and set the Scale to 100%. You've just created a template for the inner pages of your destination booklet. Save your document at this point.

6. You'll be able to see the tag-shaped templates on your document pages now. The flat-edge side of the templates (which indicates where the booklet's binding is) should be on the left-hand side of the page. If not, rotate the template until it is. Create a text box within each template box. Be sure not to make the text boxes too large! You'll want about a $1/4$-in. margin so that your text doesn't run into the booklet's binding,

8

7

6

Months to go!

or get cut off where the pages angle in or where the booklet's closure holes will be. Click inside the text boxes to insert your text. Not sure what to fill your pages with? Guests will love helpful information about the trip: where to stay, how to get there, a list of planned events, and/or points of interest. Start with an introductory page about your wedding then move on to the actual invitation details. The next pages can be devoted to a schedule of events and activities that are planned around the wedding festivities. If you're not having any formal events planned, do include descriptions of local must-see sites in your invitation booklet. Your guests will appreciate your thoughtfulness and will love having inspiration for planning their trip.

7. Save your document. If you need additional pages, go back to the blank templates that you saved in Step 5 and add text boxes and your additional text. Print the page templates onto white card stock and cut the pages out with a paper cutter or scissors. Remember to cut your pages so that they fit within the margins and binding of your booklet. That wasn't so bad, was it?

8. Once your pages are printed and cut, it is assembly time! Glue the printed pages (in the order you want them!) to the *front* of each of the booklet's inner pages. Don't glue your custom-made invite pages to the back of the chipboard booklet's pages because they won't line up! Spray adhesive or a glue stick works well (drawing B).

B.

9. To finish up the booklet, use the punch to cut out a circle from a piece of solid-colored card stock that coordinates with your color scheme. Adhere it to the center of the front cover of the booklet with a glue stick or spray adhesive. On top of the circle, attach the plastic compass (found at scrapbooking and craft stores) with the adhesive of your choice. For a special touch, punch a hole through all of the pages and covers of the booklet with a Crop-A-Dile tool and tie it shut with twine to complete the rustic travel theme.

tips & hints

- Remember, Microsoft Word is different for PCs and Macs, so if you're having problems, click on Help for assistance and to search for Watermark.

- Using a tan or brown-toned card stock will lend a vintage, weathered feel to your map printout. You could also use actual maps, too.

- If a map isn't quite your style, try using travel brochures, vintage postcards, fabric from the country of origin (think Hawaiian barkcloth or Thai silk). Certain fabrics can bleed or stain, so be sure to test the spray adhesive on a swatch of the fabric before you commit.

- Don't be afraid to play around with different embellishments to match the theme of your destination. Go for seashells for beach destinations, pine needles or twigs for the mountains, or golf tees for a sports-oriented resort.

- The best way to mail your booklet is in a padded envelope or small shipping box. Both will keep your creations safe during transportation.

Crafty Calculator

WHAT TO BUDGET

Chipboard booklet	$3.00
Card stock	$0.30
Paper	$0.20
Compass	$0.05
Twine	$0.05
Total	$3.60

COST COMPARISON

A custom-designed destination booklet from a stationer will cost upward of $10 per invitation. Our DIY version costs only $3.60 each.

STORE COST	YOUR COST
$10.00	**$3.60**

Together with their parents

Julia Esabella Sanmeters

and

Nicholas Kristoff Demett

request the honour of your presence
at their marriage
on Sunday, the fourth of March
Two thousand and twelve
at six o'clock in the evening
Mount Zion Church
11890 Leaf Avenue
Chicago, Illinois

Colorful Boxed Invitation

My dirty little secret? I buy products I have no intention of ever using just because I like the design of the box. You see, I am a sucker for great packaging. It's my weakness, my spending Achilles' heel.

Packaging design is also one of the reasons I love wedding crafts so much. Think of all of the packaging we do for weddings: the gifts, the favors, and my newest favorite packaging candidate—the wedding invitation. While the humble envelope will always have its place, sending wedding correspondence in a box adds pizzazz that an envelope can never match. This invitation is sure to wow your guests with its unexpected packaging and the surprise burst of color and dimension inside.

Time Wise

Once your invitation has been printed, you can assemble about 10 invitations in 1 hour.

Divide & Conquer

To help speed things along, get a few friends together to lend a hand with punching out the design and the final assembly of the invites.

SUPPLIES

- Rigid jewelry or mailing box, about $7^3/_8$ in. by $5^3/_8$ in. by $^3/_4$ in.
- Pink card stock, cut to about $7^1/_4$ in. by $5^1/_4$ in.
- White card stock, cut to about $7^1/_4$ in. by $5^1/_4$ in.
- Scissors
- Computer with Microsoft Word
- Printer
- Paper punch in your choice of design
- Double-sided foam tape, $^1/_4$ in. wide or larger
- Paper cutter

STATION 1: PUNCHING

Once you've finished printing out your invites, set this team to work punching holes.

STATION 2:

TAPING & LAYERING

Hand off the double-sided foam tape to this bunch. These friends are in charge of attaching the invite to the pink card stock and then adding the layers to the inside of the box.

STATION 3: FINAL ASSEMBLY

This group will address the invitations and add the postage.

DIRECTIONS

1. Before you get started with cutting and printing your invitations, it's important to measure the inside dimensions of your box. The exact measurements will vary from supplier to supplier. Use the measurements from the box you bought to determine the exact size to cut your card stock.

2. Once you have the correct inner measurements for your box, cut the pink and white card stock to size. Set the pieces aside.

3. Now it's off to the computer to create the invitation in Microsoft Word. Go to File and choose Page Setup. From the Paper Size bar, scroll down and select Manage Custom Sizes. On the bottom of the dialog box that appears, click the + button and enter the inner dimensions of your box into the field. This creates a custom page size for this project. Click OK. This will drop you back to the Page Setup menu. Click the Portrait orientation and then click OK again.

4. Since you'll be punching out designs on the left side of the invitation, you'll want to insert the invitation text on the right side of the page. To do this, create a text box on the right-hand side of the template. Adjust the size by clicking on one corner of the text box and dragging it with your mouse. Click inside the text box and insert your invitation wording. Save your document and then print it on the white card stock.

5. Using the paper punch, punch your design on the white card stock (drawing A).

6. Next, cut strips of double-sided foam tape to the inner-width measurement of your box. Turn the punched invitation over and apply foam strips to the back of the invite (drawing B). Avoid covering any punched areas with tape.

7. Set the invitation card stock on top of the pink card stock and gently press it into place, making sure the edges line up evenly on all sides (drawing C). Now place 2 strips of tape inside the box, one across the top and one along the bottom, about $^1/_4$ in. from each side.

A.   B.   C.   D.

8. To finish up the invitation, set the paper layers of the invitation into the box (drawing D). Congratulations! You're done!

tips & hints

- This box can be sent through the U.S. Postal Service without extra packaging or envelopes. Beware of shipping costs, however. Because rates change frequently at the post office, these can be quite expensive to ship in large numbers. Start by taking a sample invitation to the post office to get an estimate on shipping costs.

- Boxes of this size come in limited colors. White is the easiest to find, but there are more stylish options on the market. Check out my Resources (p. 214) for the best spots to find boxes.

- The best prices for boxes can be found when you buy in case quantities. Bought by the case, one plain white box will cost a quarter of what an individual colored box will.

- The outside of the boxes can be further customized with decorative paper, ribbon, wallpaper, wrapping paper, or even paint.

- Don't be afraid to play with different colors of invitation card stock. The best results come from using two highly contrasting colors. Patterned paper and even fabric sometimes work well as the bottom (contrast) layer. Experiment!

Crafty Calculator

WHAT TO BUDGET

Boxes, A7 size	$25.00
Card stock	$25.00
Paper punch	$ 8.00
Foam tape roll	$15.00
Total (for 50 invitations)	$73.00

COST COMPARISON

Custom boxed invitations can cost upward of $400.00 (that's $8.00 per invitation). Our DIY version costs a mere $73.00, or just $1.46 per invitation.

STORE COST	YOUR COST
$400.00	**$73.00**

Together with our parents we invite you
to share our joy and support our love
as we are exchange vows

Jessica Ackerman
and
Leopold King

Saturday, the twenty first of August
two thousand and ten
at five o'clock

Villa Montalvo
Saratoga, California

Hand-Colored Invitation

I miss crayons and coloring books. There was something so innocent and delightfully hands-on about picking up a Crayola® and just letting the color flow onto the page. No keyboards, no fancy-schmancy graphics programs. Just color and paper. Ah, I'm getting all nostalgic!

For this invitation I wanted to get us back to crafting basics. While we're a little more high-tech than a crayon, it all comes back to putting color to paper with our very own hands.

This is a great project if you're a low-tech kinda couple; on a budget; or just want a simple, beautiful way to add artistic flair to your invites. I've included my own sketch as a possible template for you to use on the invites, but you can draw or trace whatever strikes your bridal fancy!

Time Wise

Once your template is ready to go, you can complete four to six invitations in 1 hour.

Just the Two of Us

Grab your sweetheart for some crafty couple time. Not only will you breeze through the invitations in a few hours, but you'll get the satisfaction of co-creating an important part of your wedding.

SUPPLIES

- Computer with Microsoft Word
- Clip art or line drawing
  (or trace the Hand-Colored
  Invitation Template at right)
- Scanner (optional)
- Printer
- White card stock, cut to 5 in. by 7 in.
- Copic® markers in assorted colors
  to coordinate with your design

A.

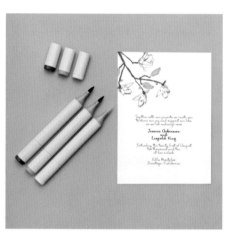

DIRECTIONS

1. Open Microsoft Word and create a new document. Go to the File and choose Page Setup. From the Paper Size bar, scroll down and select Manage Custom Sizes. On the bottom of the dialog box that appears, click the + button and enter "5 x 7" into this field. This creates a custom page size. In the fields to the right side of the dialog box, enter "7" for the height and "5" for the width. Use "0.25" for the top, bottom, left, and right margins. Click OK. This will drop you back to the Page Setup menu. Click the Portrait orientation, and then click OK again. You've just created the template for the invitation. You are awesome!

2. Now it's time to insert your invitation text and clip art onto the template. (If you've decided to use the template, simply scan and save it on your computer.) You may need to experiment with the margin settings in Word to get your clip art to the far right or left side of your page, depending on your preference. If you're a font junky like me, you'll probably spend hours playing with the look of the invitation's wording. Enjoy the process! It's fun to play around with different styles and sizes of type.

3. Once you have the wording and layout of your invitation template, save the document and print it onto your precut card stock. Print out extras in case you make a mistake or want to practice coloring before you commit to the real thing!

4. The final steps are to add color to the clip art with your Copic markers. Work in layers, one color at a time, starting with the lightest colors and moving to the darker ones (photo A).

Hand-Colored Invitation Template

Trace or reproduce this template for your invitation.

Months to go!

tips & hints

- *Remember, Microsoft Word is different for PCs and Macs, so if you're having problems, click on Help for assistance.*

- *Copic markers are alcohol-based pens that allow you to add color without streaks or blotches. They're low-odor and refillable, and are most often used by comic book artists and graphic designers. It takes time to get the hang of them, so practice coloring with them on scratch paper before you start on your invitations.*

- *Any open-lined drawing will work well for this project. Check out the Resources (p. 214) for the best places to find ready-to-color clip art.*

- *Most heavy card stock will work for this project, but watercolor papers are also an option. You can find this paper at nearly every arts and craft store in pads or packages at reasonable prices. All you will have to do is cut it to size.*

Crafty Calculator

WHAT TO BUDGET

Card stock	$30.00
Copic markers (5)	$30.00
Total (for 100 invitations)	$60.00

COST COMPARISON

Copic markers can be quite expensive, but will last you through an entire set of invitations. Expect to pay around $6.00 per marker, which prices out to only $60.00 for 100 complete invitations. Custom-designed hand-colored invitations cost upward of $300.00 for 100 invites from stationers.

STORE COST	YOUR COST
$300.00	**$60.00**

Together with their parents
Isabella Valenchez
and
Craig McDermott
request the honour of your presence
at their marriage
on Saturday, the 10th of August
Two thousand and ten
at six o'clock in the evening
Unity Church
12345 Main Street
Pasadena, California

Dry Embossed Invitation

I am hopelessly addicted to embossed stationery. There's something so wonderfully delightful about designs that are pressed into the paper. Maybe it's how the raised surface makes the invitation more tactile or perhaps it's just the sophistication of tone-on-tone design. Whatever it is, embossed invites have an extra-special something of "ooh la la!" proportions.

This project requires a special tool called an embossing or die-cutting machine. I personally love the Cuttlebug because of its compact size, user friendliness, and affordable price, but there are several different makes and models on the market to suit your fancy. With most, you can use embossing folders from competing manufacturers (check with the manufacturer before you buy). Some scrapbook stores offer in-store die-cutting or embossing machine rental. If you're on the fence about buying a machine, ask in your local

Time Wise

Once your invites are printed, you can expect to emboss anywhere from 20 to 40 cards in 1 hour.

A Little Me Time

This solo project is great for a weekend afternoon. You'll be using some muscle power with the crank handle, so put on your high-energy playlist for inspiration.

SUPPLIES

- Computer with Microsoft Word
- Printer
- Card stock, cut to 5 in. by 7 in.
- Embossing or die-cutting machine
  (I recommend the Cuttlebug)
- Embossing folder

A.

B.

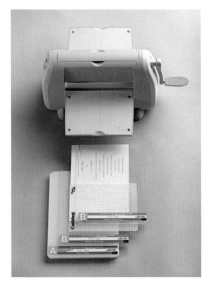

shops to see if there is one available for customers to use. That way you can try out the embossing machine and decide if the crafty accessory is right for you.

DIRECTIONS

Before you get started, it's worth noting that each die-cutting or embossing machine has its own set of standard parts. These directions are written for the Cuttlebug. Other machines work in a similar fashion, but the exact materials and steps may differ slightly. Definitely read the manual for your machine for specific instructions on its use before beginning.

1. Let's get started by creating your printed invitation. Open a new Word document. Go to File and choose Page Setup. From the Paper Size bar, scroll down and select Manage Custom Sizes. On the bottom of the dialog box that appears, click the + button and enter "5 x 7" into this field. This creates a custom page size. In the fields to the right side of the dialog box, enter "5" for the height and "7" for the width. Use "0.25" for the top, bottom, left, and right margins. Click OK. This will drop you back to the Page Setup menu. Click the Landscape orientation, and then click OK again. You now have a template for a 5-in. by 7-in. invitation.

2. Because you'll be embossing the left half of the invitation, you'll want to print only on the right side. The easiest way to do this is to create a text box on the right-hand side of the template.

3. Click inside the text box and insert your invitation wording. Save your document and then print onto the card stock.

4. Now we get to emboss! Open your embossing folder and slip in one of the printed invitations so that the *unprinted*, left-hand side of the invite is aligned where you'd like the textured design to appear (photo A). Be certain to emboss only the space to the left of the invitation's text even if the invite does

not fill up the entire width of the embossing folder. Close the folder. Be careful here—the invitation could move around when you close the folder.

5. Next, layer the closed embossing folder between two B cutting pads. Set the stack on top of the A cutting pad, and place the entire stack on the shelf of the Cuttlebug (photo B).

6. Press the stack through the machine using the crank handle (photo C), and then disassemble the stack and pull out your finished invitation.

C.

tips & hints

- *Remember, Microsoft Word is different for PCs and Macs, so if you're having problems, click on Help for assistance.*

- *Any color card stock can be used for the invitation. Darker colors often show embossing better than lighter ones, but the ink from your printer may not show up as well.*

- *Embossing folders are available in dozens of designs. Embossing folders and plates made by one company often work in die-cutting machines made by other companies.*

- *If you're short on time, emboss precut or preprinted invitations from your local stationer.*

- *Embossing isn't just for invitations! You can emboss paper napkins, programs, menus, favor boxes, thank-you cards—nearly anything you can fit in the embossing machine.*

- *Craft stores often have great deals on specialty items. If you're investing in an embossing machine, keep an eye out for coupon offers from local stores—some offer 40 to 50 percent off!*

Crafty Calculator

WHAT TO BUDGET

Cuttlebug machine	$60.00
Embossing folder	$ 5.00
Card stock	$ 10.00
Total (for 100 invites)	$75.00

COST COMPARISON

Custom letter-pressed or embossed invitations can cost anywhere from $3.00 to $10.00 per set—a small fortune for most couples. This DIY embossed invitation costs about $0.75 per invitation. Irresistible!

STORE COST	YOUR COST
$10.00	**75¢**

Lace Flower-Girl's Basket

If your family is like mine (pack rats), there are bound to be plenty of delightful but neglected crochet or lace doilies lurking in someone's china hutch or attic. These are wedding treasures waiting to be unleashed, I tell you.

Once relegated to covering grandma's coffee table or chair arms, the humble and oh-so-retro doily can now be transformed into something adorable—and useful—for your wedding: a flower-girl's basket. With just a few supplies, you can turn a doily into an heirloom wedding item that you'll be able to pass on for generations to come.

Using liquid fabric stiffener to coat the doily allows you to mold it into a three-dimensional shape to hold flower petals, gift cards, favors, or

8 7 6

Months to go!

Time Wise

Securing the ribbon to the basket is a snap and should only take 5 minutes or so, but allow the doily basket to dry completely before you add this finishing touch.

•

A Little Me Time

It's best to go it alone on this very simple project.

SUPPLIES

- Bowl for shaping the basket
- Aluminum foil
- Newspaper
- Liquid fabric stiffener, found at craft stores
- Crochet or lace doily, 8-in. diameter or larger
- Ribbon, about 12 in., in a width that will fit through the doily's holes
- Scissors

other wedding goodies. This project is very simple, but do make sure to start it at least 48 hours before you need to use the basket so that the doily has ample time to dry and take shape. Give the ribbon you plan to use a test run to be certain it will fit through the holes in the doily.

DIRECTIONS

1. This super-easy project involves molding a piece of fabric into the shape of an inverted bowl. To get started, cover an upside-down bowl with a layer of aluminum foil.

2. Next, spread out the newspaper on your work area. Pour liquid fabric stiffener over your doily. Make sure the entire doily is fully saturated with the stiffener. Wring out any excess onto a few sheets of newspaper and toss them out.

3. Place the wet doily on top of the foil-covered bowl. Smooth out any wrinkles (drawing A).

A.

4. Let the doily dry overnight on the overturned bowl.

5. Remove the dry doily from the bowl. Sometimes the foil will stick to the fabric a bit. Don't worry about it. Any bits of foil will pull off pretty easily.

6. You should now have a perfect bowl-shaped basket! Your last step is to cut a length of ribbon for a handle and tie each end to the basket. Make sure that you can hold the basket by the handle and that it stays level. About 12 in. of ribbon should be sufficient, depending on how big your basket is.

7. On the Big Day, fill the basket with petals and let your adorable flower girl loose down the aisle.

tips & hints

- *This project is an excellent way to use heirloom pieces of fabric. Vintage wedding gowns, hankies, veils . . . nearly any fabric will work. Do beware that the fabric stiffener will stain silks darker and will most likely shrink wools.*

- *Bowls aren't the only molds you can use. Be oh-so-clever by using unusually shaped cake pans, pumpkins or gourds, vases, or other nifty objects. Intricate details often don't work well, so choose bold, smooth shapes.*

- *Ribbon can be woven through the holes in the doilies for added pizzazz.*

- *If you make a mistake with the mold or just don't like it, simply wash the fabric stiffener out of the doily and start over. (Don't you love mistake-proof projects?)*

Crafty Calculator

WHAT TO BUDGET

Doily	$ 8.00
Fabric stiffener	$ 3.00
Ribbon	$ 2.00
Total	$ 13.00

COST COMPARISON

Lace and crochet flower-girl's baskets can cost upward of $30.00 in bridal salons. This great little DIY version costs about $13.00 to create at home, and the price is cut in half if you use a doily that you already own!

STORE COST	YOUR COST
$30.00	**$13.00**

Months to go!

Memorial Candle

One of the most requested project ideas I get at DIYBride.com is for unobtrusive ways to honor deceased relatives. Many couples, by superstition or tact, don't wish to bring up the deaths of loved ones or take away from the joy of the day, but they do wish to pay respects to their family and friends who've passed away. So, how do you pull this off with grace and subtlety?

One of my favorite solutions is to use a memorial candle as an alternative to the unity candle ceremony. Another use is to display the candle (or candles) as the centerpiece on a special memorial table set up at the ceremony or reception.

This is a deceptively easy project. While it's harder than it looks, it is within the skills of

Time Wise

This super-easy project can be completed in under 1 hour.

•

A Little Me Time

This is an after-work, throw-on-your-sweats-and-get-comfy solo project. Calming classical music might put you in the right frame of mind.

SUPPLIES
- Scanned photograph
- Translucent vellum paper, available at craft and scrapbook supply stores
- Scissors
- Heat embossing tool
- White pillar candle, 8-in. circumference, with smooth surface
- Waxed paper

newbie and seasoned crafters alike. What you'll be doing is slightly melting the surface of a candle and then pressing a vellum print onto the candle's tacky surface. The print will fuse to the candle, creating a seamless image. The hardest part is to melt the candle enough to affix the image without misshaping it.

DIRECTIONS

1. To get started, print a photograph of the loved one onto a piece of vellum. Make sure the photo is not taller than your candle. Let the image dry completely, at least 30 minutes.

2. Cut the photograph out of the vellum, leaving at least a ¼-in. border around all sides of the image.

3. With the heat embossing tool, begin heating the candle's surface (photo A). Hold the tool 3 in. to 4 in. from the candle. You'll see the wax become shiny as it heats—this is what you're aiming for.

A.

B.

4. Working quickly, press the vellum picture onto the melted wax, making sure the photo is oriented correctly (photo B). It should bond to the candle almost immediately.

5. Wrap the candle in a length of waxed paper and roll the candle on a smooth flat surface. This will press the image into the candle and prevent the candle from losing its shape.

6. If you have areas of the vellum that aren't fused to the candle, that's okay. Just remove the waxed paper and reapply heat, then roll the candle again until the picture sets into the wax.

tips & hints

- The heat embossing tools gets super hot. Watch those fingers and keep any flammable materials away from your work area.

- It's okay to work in sections if you need to. Sometimes the wax cools too fast to do a whole candle circumference at once.

- As a general safety rule, do not leave the candle unattended while it's burning. There's little chance that the vellum will catch fire because it's embedded in the wax, but it's better to be on the safe side.

Crafty Calculator

WHAT TO BUDGET

Candle	$4.00
Vellum (per sheet)	$0.30
Total	$4.30

COST COMPARISON

Custom memorial candles can be outrageously expensive. Specialty retailers charge around $35.00 for a medium-size candle. This DIY version costs just $4.30.

STORE COST	YOUR COST
$35.00	$4.30

Wire Bird's-Nest Ring Pillow

Hello, urban nature lover! You and I are kindred spirits. We both share a love of the outdoors but also have a deep appreciation for contemporary design. One of my favorite things to do is combine modern materials with organic shapes, turning things of nature into pieces of chic art.

When one of my DIYBride.com members asked if I could develop something "bird themed with a modern twist," I just knew I had to make a bird's-nest ring pillow out of metal wire. This became one of my favorite projects of the year and was a hit with my new bride friend.

The scale of the nest can be altered to fit the hands of your particular ring bearer. This one was

Time Wise

While this is a simple project, allow yourself at least 1 hour to complete it.

•

A Little Me Time

This is a great project to tackle when sitting in front of the TV after a long day at work.

SUPPLIES

- 10 to 15 yds. of 26-gauge silver wire, for a small/medium nest
- Wire cutters
- Assortment of beads
- Needle-nose pliers
- Swatch of fabric, about 3 in. in diameter to line the inside of the nest

created for very small hands, measuring about 3 in. wide. By adjusting the amount of wire and tension you use, you can easily make adjustments to best fit your needs.

DIRECTIONS

1. Unwind 5 to 10 yd. of wire from the spool. With your fingers, straighten the wire out to remove any twists or bumps along the length.

2. Now you are ready to make the nest's base. Wrap the wire loosely around your index finger 5 to 10 times, leaving a 1-in. tail (drawing A). At the end of the project, you'll attach beads to the tail (which will be at the bottom of the nest) as added decoration.

3. Now begin wrapping the remaining wire around the nest's base you just created, stopping every few feet to slip a bead onto the wire. As you wrap the wire, it's important to weave it between layers (drawing B). If you go for a straight spiral coil, the wire will just unwind. Varying the tension on your layers by alternately making the wire tighter or looser as you wrap it helps create a disheveled look—like a real bird's nest—and allows room to slip the wire loops under and around each other.

4. Place the fabric swatch in the center of the nest so that your rings will have a lovely place to sit on their way down the aisle.

5. To finish the nest, attach a bead to the 1-in. tail you made in step 2 (drawing C). Using a pair of needle-nose pliers, make an open hook at the end of the tail piece. Slip a large bead or crystal onto the hook and then close the loop with the pliers. Now, how cute is that!

A.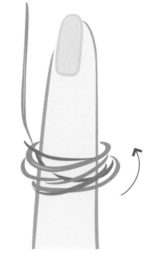

B.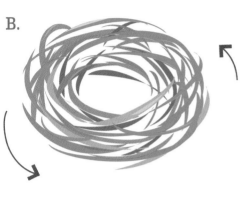

C.

tips & hints

- *The more wire you use, the bigger and bulkier the nest will be.*

- *Conversely, the tighter you wrap the wire, the smaller the nest will be.*

- *Silver or gold wire (or both!) can be used for this project.*

- *While this project may seem incredibly easy, it can be a challenge. Holding onto the wire with one hand while wrapping with another can get unwieldy as you start building bulk. Having a friend (or fiancé) around to lend an extra hand will be helpful, but you can do it on your own with some patience.*

Crafty Calculator

WHAT TO BUDGET

Wire	$6.00
Beads	$2.00
Total	$8.00

COST COMPARISON

I haven't seen anything like this on the market yet, which means *you* get to be a trendsetter! Custom ring pillows can cost $40.00 to more than $100.00 at specialty shops. Our great little ring nest will cost you about $8.00 to make at home.

STORE COST	YOUR COST
$100.00	**$8.00**

5

4

3

Months to go!

5-3 Months to Go!

ACCESSORIES WITH YOUR SENSE OF STYLE

Are you feeling the timeline crunch yet? In fewer than 20 Saturdays you'll be married! Not to worry. Here, you'll find a mix of very cool, very budget-friendly must-have projects that can be completed in a day or two. By now you've probably ordered your gown. Why not make a few to-die-for accessories to go with it and save hundreds of dollars in the process? This chapter is devoted to gorgeous accoutrements that are easy to make and easy on your checkbook, plus there's a great idea for a bachelorette party invite (think relaxing spa!).

Bridal Headband

While some friends and colleagues may accuse me of being a wedding-supply pack rat, I like to think of myself as an eco-friendly, recycled-art champion. Give to me your outdated doohickeys, your abundant overstock, your unwanted wedding and craft swag! For one of my biggest thrills is taking an overlooked hand-me-down item and turning it into a cherished heirloom.

While searching through my box of jewelry goodness, looking for an accessories project idea for this book, I spied an overly ornate costume necklace and thought, "Ugh! That's too gaudy to wear around anyone's neck! But, hey, with a little crafty finesse it'd make a gorgeous headband."

Time Wise

Set aside 1 hour or so to complete this project after you've picked out the jewelry you'll be using. For best results, let the adhesive dry overnight before you wear the tiara.

A Little Me Time

Decompress after a long day by grabbing your jewelry finds, turning on your fave playlist, and letting the creative juices flow.

SUPPLIES

- Plain gold-tone or silver-tone metal headband, available at millinery supply shops
- Necklace or accessories of your choice
- Wire cutters
- Jewelry file, found at craft and bead shops
- Jewelry epoxy or hot glue
- Clothespins

This headband project could easily be adapted to nearly any kind of jewelry that has a flat back and a bit of bend to it. Rhinestone or plastic earrings, bracelets, and necklaces all work well as headband decoration material. Strings of pearls? Not so much because they don't have enough surface area to get a good grab on the headband base.

DIRECTIONS

1. The first step is the most time-consuming one. You'll need to prep your jewelry pieces so that they will both fit the headband size and stick to the band's surface when glued in place. Start by inspecting all of the jewelry you intend to use for flaws you can't live with, and lay the keepers out around the top of the headband to get an idea of the placement. If the necklace is larger than the headband, use wire cutters to clip the jewelry to size. Using a jewelry file, rough up the top surface of the headband and the back side of the necklace. This will help the pieces bond later on during the gluing process.

2. If you're using a necklace, multiple necklaces, or an assortment of jewelry items, it's likely you'll want to remove extra chains, connector rings, earring backings, or other non-decorative parts from the pieces. Your wire cutters are excellent for this task. Just snip away anything you don't want and file the rough edges with the jewelry file until they're smooth.

A.

3. You've just completed the hardest part of this project. Good job! Now, it's time to glue the jewelry pieces to the headband (drawing A). Which glue to use? It depends on the jewelry. If you're using newer costume jewelry, you'll most likely be safe with hot glue. Older pieces made of glass or rhinestone costume jewelry will usually require the use of a jewelry epoxy. Vintage rhinestones may change color or even flake or burst under the heat of hot glue, so if you aren't sure what you've got, stick with the epoxy. New rhinestone jewelry tends to be more resilient. If you're using pieces with Bakelite® or other plastic-like materials, I recommend using low-temperature hot glue. Sometimes epoxies can have a bad chemical reaction with plastics. Your best bet is to apply glue to a test piece of jewelry before assembling the entire headband.

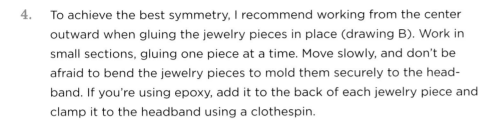

B.

4. To achieve the best symmetry, I recommend working from the center outward when gluing the jewelry pieces in place (drawing B). Work in small sections, gluing one piece at a time. Move slowly, and don't be afraid to bend the jewelry pieces to mold them securely to the headband. If you're using epoxy, add it to the back of each jewelry piece and clamp it to the headband using a clothespin.

5. Let the adhesive dry according to the manufacturer's instructions. That's all there is to it!

tips & hints

- *Don't be afraid to mix and match different materials for this project. Think about using Grandma's old brooches or buttons from your mom's wedding gown or cuff links from all of the men in your family.*

- *Symmetry is overrated! Be daring and cluster a group of beautiful jewelry pieces on the side of your headband. It makes a dramatic statement.*

- *Try on your headband before you start adding jewelry to it. Very few metal headbands will be comfortable right out of the box, so don't be shy about bending and stretching it to accommodate your head size.*

- *If a headband isn't your thing, this project can easily be done with a metal hair comb or barrette.*

Crafty Calculator

WHAT TO BUDGET

Metal headband	$ 6.00
Necklace	$12.00
Epoxy/glue	$ 4.00
Jewelry file	$ 5.00
Total	$27.00

COST COMPARISON

Ornate headbands at bridal salons can cost $65.00 or more. Ours, using a store-bought necklace, costs way less at $27.00. If you use found or heirloom jewelry, you'll save even more.

STORE COST	YOUR COST
$65.00	**$27.00**

Months to go!

5
4
3

Bridesmaid Button Hairpin

Finding unique, heartfelt, and affordable gifts for your hard-to-please maids can seem like the quest for the Holy Grail when you're working with a tight timeline and an even tighter budget. Fear not, my lovelies! I have an adorable adornment project that's sure to be a hit with even your quirkiest of bridesmaids. These sweet hairpins take just a minute to make and can be customized to fit the style and personality of each of your dearest girlfriends.

Before you get started, I shall send you on a hunt for button awesomeness. Scour fabric stores, secondhand shops, and even Grandma's sewing

Time Wise

Once you've located the perfect buttons, you can create 2 to 3 hairpins in under 30 minutes.

•

A Little Me Time

This super-simple solo project is ideal for a quiet afternoon listening to tunes or after dinner while catching up on your favorite TV shows. Who knew multitasking could be so wonderfully relaxing?

SUPPLIES

- Waxed paper
- Hot glue gun and glue sticks
- Buttons, new or vintage
- Wire cutters or very sharp scissors
- File (metal nail file or a wood file)
- Hairpins, found at drugstores and beauty supply shops
- Scissors or craft knife

A.

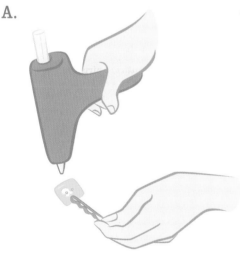

room for one-of-a-kind buttons to use in the project. Some of my favorite button finds have come from vintage garments. The best button candidates are under 1 in. in diameter and are fairly lightweight, to keep the hairpins comfortable for the wearer.

DIRECTIONS

1. Place waxed paper on your work surface to protect it from hot glue spills. (Waxed paper makes for easy clean up and resists burning.)

2. Insert a glue stick into your glue gun, plug in the gun, and turn it on to start heating, making sure it's sitting on the protected area of your table.

3. Examine the buttons. If the buttons have little tabs on the back, you'll need to remove them to create a flat surface to attach the hairpin. Use wire cutters (or super-sharp scissors) and cut the tab off as close to the base of the button as you can. If there are sharp edges left after the cut, use a file (a metal nail file will usually do, but sometimes a wood file is needed) to smooth out the bumps.

4. Next, glue the hairpin to the back of the button. Simply apply a small dot of hot glue to the button, and then quickly press the flat side of the hairpin into the glue (drawing A). Hold it there for a few seconds until the glue hardens a bit. There will likely be excess glue on the back of the button. This can be trimmed away with a sharp pair of scissors or craft knife after the glue has cooled. You now have a finished hairpin, you crafty goddess!

tips & hints

- I adore using vintage buttons for this project. Scour tag, jumble, and garage sales for unique finds. eBay® can also be a wonderful source for buttons.

- Fabric and craft stores carry tons of interesting new buttons. If you want to match your bridesmaids' dress color, using new buttons may be your best bet.

- For something totally unique, layer different colored and shaped buttons on the hairpin.

- Beware of foil-backed buttons. They can discolor under the heat of the hot glue.

- Keep a glass of ice water nearby when you're working on this project. Hot glue is seriously hot and can cause nasty burns. It's likely that you will touch the molten glue at some point during this project, and the cold water will help soothe your skin.

Crafty Calculator

WHAT TO BUDGET

Hairpins (for 20)	$2.00
Buttons (for 2)	$2.00
Total (per pair)	$2.20

COST COMPARISON

Fun and fabulous button hairpins can be found online and in boutiques for around $7.00 each. This DIY version costs a mere $2.00 for a pair and can be done even cheaper if you use found or freebie buttons.

STORE COST	YOUR COST
$7.00	**$2.20**

Embellished Bridal Wrap

hough I'm certain your shoulders are quite lovely, you hottie bride you, some houses of worship aren't quite so keen on letting you flaunt bare skin at the altar no matter how uber-gorgeous your gown may be. So, how do you modest it up without sacrificing your style or breaking your budget?

The answer is a wrap. Simply embellished with pretty flowers and crystals, this shawl is subtle enough that it won't compete with your gown and offers enough coverage to pass the modesty requirements of most churches. Even better? You can create one in under 1 hour and for less than $20.00.

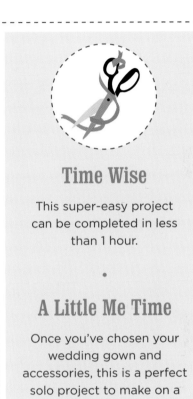

Time Wise

This super-easy project can be completed in less than 1 hour.

A Little Me Time

Once you've chosen your wedding gown and accessories, this is a perfect solo project to make on a quiet afternoon.

SUPPLIES

- Iron
- Chiffon scarf or wrap, about 15 in. by 60 in.
- Silk flowers, 25 to 50, depending on the flower size and amount you want to use
- Crystal beads, 6 mm to 8 mm, one per flower
- Hot glue gun with glue sticks and fabric glue sticks

DIRECTIONS

1. This project is so wonderfully easy! In just minutes you'll be done, so let's get started. Iron the scarf on your iron's lowest setting to remove any wrinkles.

2. Remove the silk flower buds from the stems and set them aside.

3. With the glue gun, put a small dollop of glue into the center of a flower and quickly place a crystal on the glue (photo A). Be extra careful here. The glue will be very hot! Watch those fingers. Repeat for each flower. Unplug the glue gun and remove the glue stick. Replace it with a glue stick for fabric.

A.

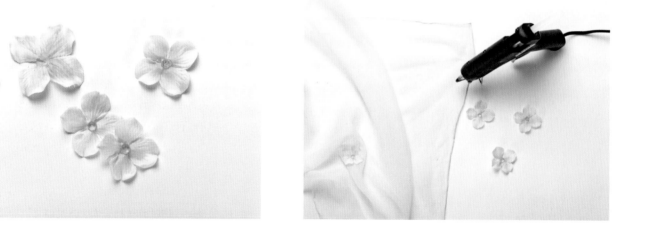

B.

4. Once you've added dazzle to your flowers, it's time to attach them to the wrap. Lay the silk wrap on a flat surface and place the flowers randomly over the surface. Play around with the placement to get a scattered effect.

5. Once you are happy with the flower placement, use fabric hot glue to secure the flowers to the wrap (photo B). Use very small amounts of glue. Big globs of glue will show through the back of the scarf and may bleed out of the sides.

tips & hints

- This would make a lovely gift for the bridesmaids, flower girls, or moms. Use different fabrics to match or coordinate with their gowns.

- While you can use any silk flower you'd like, fewer and smaller are generally better. Too many flowers or really big ones can make the wrap too heavy both physically and visually.

- Rhinestones can be used in place of crystals for a little extra sparkle.

- Don't be afraid to play around with placement of the flowers. While the random, scattered look is pretty, creating your own patterns and designs can be a lot of fun.

- Other fabrics that work well for this project: silk and polyester shantung, tulle (think bridal veils), velvet, and silk-wool blends.

Crafty Calculator

WHAT TO BUDGET

Scarf	$4.00
Flowers	$5.00
Crystals	$4.00
Glue	$4.00
Total	$17.00

COST COMPARISON

High-end bridal shawls at bridal salons go for $150.00 or more. Our version costs just around 10 percent of that, and you get a custom-made accessory for your big day.

STORE COST	YOUR COST
$150.00	$17.00

Ribbon & Lace Bridal Slipper

When you've just blown the equivalent of a small country's gross national product on your to-die-for gown of gowns, not just any bridal shoe will do. The problem? You're now short on cash and plain, off-the-shelf discount heels are your only afford-able option.

Not to worry! With this crafty shoe makeover, we can get you set up with couture kicks in just a few short minutes. Using lace, ribbon, embellishments, and a bit of glue, you'll have a pair of gorgeous designer bridal shoes that'll dazzle everyone in your path as you strut down that aisle.

This project doesn't require a lot of exact measurements, a sure blessing for those of you

Time Wise

Set aside at least 4 hours for the shoe makeover. You'll need 1 hour or so to add decorations, and you should let the fabric glue dry fully for a few hours (or overnight).

•

A Little Me Time

Designing Cinderella-worthy footwear deserves all your attention. Grab a few of your favorite mags for inspiration and let your inner fashionista fly solo on this one.

SUPPLIES

- Lace, about 1 yd., width depends on how much of the underlying shoe to leave exposed
- Scissors
- 1 pair of unembellished satin or silk shoes
- Foam brush
- Fabric glue
- Paper towels
- $1/4$-in.-wide satin ribbon for the bows, about 1 yd.
- 2 rhinestone buttons
- Hot glue gun and glue sticks

who prefer to "eyeball" for symmetry or are ruler-phobic. See? I do read all of those "please don't make me measure anything" e-mails from my DIY-bride friends.

DIRECTIONS

1. To get started, cut the yard of lace in half and lay one of the lengths over the top of one of the shoes. Move it around to find the best position that'll cover the part of the shoe you'd like to adorn. Use sharp scissors to cut the lace to the shape of the shoe, leaving about a $1/4$-in. overlap of lace on all sides that you will either trim away later or tuck into the shoe (drawing A). Repeat this step for the other shoe.

2. If your piece of lace is going to the top edge of the shoe, as shown in the photo on p. 102, the $1/4$-in. overlap of lace will be folded over the top of the shoe's edge and adhered to the inside of the shoe when it comes time to glue. If there are any notches or cutouts on the shoe, you'll need to trim the lace to fit those contours with a pair of sharp scissors.

3. Using a foam brush, apply fabric glue to one side of the lace pieces (drawing B). Press the sticky side of the lace down onto the surface of the shoe (drawing C). Use a damp paper towel to wipe away any excess glue that may seep through from under the lace.

4. If the lace meets the sole of your shoe, it's important to press the lace as far into the crease between the shoe and its sole for maximum adhesion. Trim away any excess lace and allow the fabric glue to completely dry. (Check the instructions on the glue bottle for the recommended drying time.)

5. Once the lace is in place and dry, you can now go wild (or mild, if that's your style) with the embellishments. This is the fun part! For the shoes in the photo, I created a simple bow from satin ribbon for each shoe and then I used my hot glue gun and attached a pretty rhinestone button to the center of the bow (drawing D). And then I glued the blinged-out bow to the shoe (drawing E). Voilà! Instant couture on the cheap.

A.

B.

C.

D.

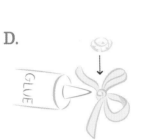

E.

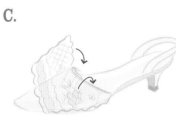

tips & hints

- The simpler the design of the shoe, the easier it'll be to embellish. Look for styles that have no embroidery, rhinestones, or fancy cutouts on the upper part of the shoe.

- Nearly any lightweight fabric can be used to adorn the shoe instead of lace. Don't be afraid to be daring with brightly colored satins, embroidered silks, or off-the-beaten-path cotton prints.

- Beware! Some fabrics change color when they come in contact with fabric adhesive. Test out a small swatch with your glue before you decide to attach it to the shoe.

- Can't think of any fun embellishments? How about vintage buttons, costume jewelry (clip-on earrings are wonderful for this application), lockets, rhinestones, Grandpa's cuff links, or silk flowers?

Crafty Calculator

WHAT TO BUDGET

Satin bridal shoes	$25.00
Lace	$ 4.00
Glue	$ 4.00
Buttons	$ 5.00
Ribbon	$ 3.00
Total	$ 41.00

COST COMPARISON

Designer bridal shoes can cost a small fortune at boutiques. Expect to pay around $100.00 for a simple, embellished pair of bridal pumps from a mid-range designer. Our pair cost $41.00, but depending on the choice of discount heels, they can cost well under that.

STORE COST	YOUR COST
$100.00	**$41.00**

5
4
3
Months to go!

Feather Boutonniere

Just recently I had dinner with my friend Matt, and he was lamenting how his ultra-feminine bride-to-be wanted him to wear *flowers* on his suit at their wedding. It took me a second to figure out he was talking about a boutonniere. "It's pretty standard groomswear, Matt. What's wrong with a simple rose or lily boutonniere?" I asked. "Too girly," he replied. When I asked him what he thought would be a suitable alternate? "Something manly! Fishing tackle! Car parts! Fuzzy dice! A skull and crossbones!" Ah, romance.

I made it my mission to come up with a stylish boutonniere option that would appeal to fashion-conscious brides without threatening the masculinity of their grooms. Instead of using flowers, I opted for something more natural and organic—

Time Wise

This super-easy project can be made in under 1 hour.

•

A Little Me Time

Got a few minutes to spare? Grab your supplies and plop yourself in front of the TV. You'll be done with this project before your favorite sitcom ends.

SUPPLIES

- Assorted feathers, available in bunches at craft and millinery stores
- Floral tape
- 1 crystal bead, 6 mm
- 22-gauge wire, about 8 in.
- Scissors or craft knife
- ¼-in.-wide velvet ribbon, about 6 in.
- Hot glue gun and glue sticks
- Corsage pin

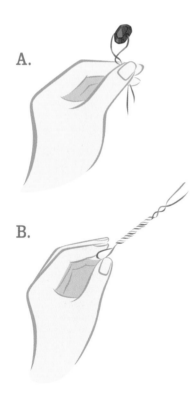

A.

B.

feathers as the base of the boutonniere with a just a little sparkle added via a crystal bead. Tied off with a velvet ribbon, this stunning boutonniere is a gorgeous (but still dude-worthy) accessory any groom will be proud to sport down the aisle.

DIRECTIONS

1. Gather a group of 4 to 6 feathers of different shapes and sizes (from 4 in. to 7 in. long) into a mini-bouquet. Arrange them with the tallest feathers in the back and the shorter feathers in front. Don't be afraid to play around with placement and sizes of the feathers in this step to get a look you (and your groom) like.

2. Bind the feathers together with a few wraps of floral tape to keep your boutonniere arrangement intact. You needn't cover the entire stem of the boutonniere yet.

3. The next step is to create a crystal stem for added boutonniere bling. Place the crystal bead on the length of wire, then fold the wire in half so that the bead is in the middle (drawing A). Holding the crystal in place with one hand, use your other hand to twist the wire ends tightly around each other (drawing B).

4. Place the crystal stem in the front of the feathers in the boutonniere and bind it in place with more floral tape (drawing C). Cover the entire bottom area of the boutonniere with floral tape to create a single stem. Ideally, the stem will be about 3 in. long when complete. If it's any longer, use sharp scissors or a craft knife to trim it to size.

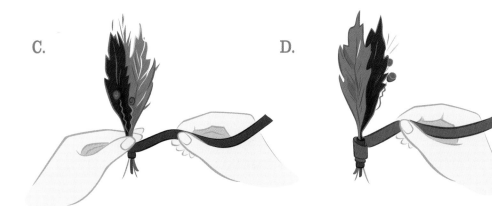

C.   D.

5. Cover the floral tape stem with velvet ribbon, working in a tight spiral from top to bottom, then bottom to top (drawing D). Secure the ribbon to itself with a bit of hot glue.

6. When it's time to walk down the aisle, pin the boutonniere to the groom's suit or tuxedo with a corsage pin.

tips & hints

- Feathers are available in nearly any color and size, making it easy to match the season or style of your wedding.

- Trimming feathers to a smaller size or even a different shape can be done by using very sharp scissors. Dull blades will usually cut unevenly.

- If ribbon is too froufrou for your guy, try wrapping the stem with twine, raffia, or leather to lend a more masculine vibe.

Crafty Calculator

WHAT TO BUDGET

Feather assortment	$ 6.00
Floral tape	$ 2.00
Crystal bead	$ 0.20
Wire	$ 3.00
Ribbon	$ 3.00
Total (for 3 boutonnieres)	$14.20

COST COMPARISON

The supplies listed here can make three boutonnieres (though you'll have to buy more crystals), making this a very economical project. Custom-designed feather boutonnieres can set you back $25.00 or more from higher-end salons. You get yours for $4.73 and not a penny more!

STORE COST	YOUR COST
$25.00	**$4.73**

Day Spa Bachelorette Party Invite

In the midst of the craziness that is wedding planning will come a day when everything comes to a screeching halt for one extra-special event: your bachelorette party. Once relegated to wild–night–on–the–town drunken brouhahas, the bachelorette party is becoming more of a civilized soiree. No more embarrassing marital aid–themed props and silly games. It's all about celebrating *you* with pampering and stress-free fun with your best girlfriends at a chic day spa or your favorite spot for tea. It's good to be girly! Don't be shy about reveling in it.

This modern, feminine bachelorette party invitation is one you can be proud of sending to your lucky invitees. The bold colors and fun patterns

Time Wise

Once your template is created, you can finish about 12 invites in 1 hour.

•

It's a Girl Thing

Strict etiquette dictates that you not plan your own bachelorette party or shower, but don't let that stop you from lending a hand to your less-crafty girlfriends if they need help. Otherwise, pass this project off to your bridesmaids and take a well-earned break.

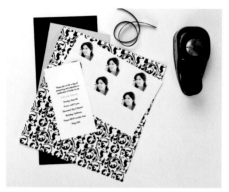

stand out from the other pink and pastel options for brides-to-be, plus it's personalized with a photo of your gorgeous self. You won't find that at your local card supply store! And it's also perfect as a shower or bridesmaid's luncheon invite. The unusual size adds visual interest and saves on costs for the hostess, too.

SUPPLIES
- Computer with Microsoft Word
- Bride's photo, about 1½ in. in diameter
- White card stock, 8½ in. by 11 in.
- Printer
- 1⅜-in. circle punch
- White card stock, 3 in. by 6 in.
- Double-sided tape
- Black card stock, 12½ in. by 3 in.
- Bone folder
- Patterned paper, 5 in. by 1 in.
- Yellow card stock, 5 in. by 2 in.
- ¼-in.-wide grosgrain ribbon, about 6 in.

DIRECTIONS

1. To get started with this invitation, begin by printing out a picture of the bride. You'll need one image per invite, but you should be able to fit 6 photos on a single sheet of 8½-in. by 11-in. white card stock. Open Microsoft Word and create a new document. From the toolbar, select Insert, then Picture. You'll be prompted to select the photo from your hard drive or other source. Find the photo and click Insert. You'll then be able to double-click the photo and change the dimensions through a pop-up menu. Because you'll be punching out each of the photos with a 1⅜-in. circle punch, you'll want the picture to be slightly larger than that—about 1½ in. in diameter—to avoid any white or unprinted areas when you punch the image out.

2. Click the resized photo to select it. Copy and paste the photo multiple times onto the page. Save your document and print it onto the white card stock.

3. Using the circle punch, punch out the pictures of the bride (photo A). Set aside.

4. Now it's time to create the written invitation in Microsoft Word. Go to File and choose Page Setup. From the Paper Size bar, scroll down and select Manage Custom Sizes. On the bottom of the dialog box that appears, click the + button and enter "3 x 6" into this field. This creates a custom page size. In the fields on the right side of the dialog box, enter "6" for the height and "3" for the width. Use "0.25" for the top, bottom, left, and right margins. Click OK. This will drop you back to the Page Setup menu. Click the Portrait orientation, and then click OK. You now have a template for your invitation.

A.

B.

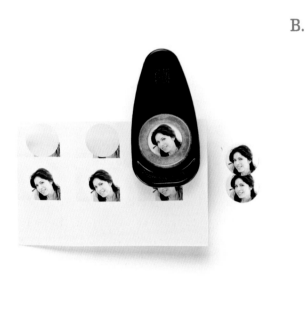

Please join us for a day of
pampering and relaxation in
celebration of bride-to-be

Gabriella Galeazzi

Sunday, June 06

10 a.m. until 4 p.m.

Claremont Spa & Resort

Berkeley, California

Please RSVP no later than

May 20th

5. Insert your invitation text into the document. Save your document, and print it onto the 3-in. by 6-in. white card stock. Take the 12-in. by 3-in. black card stock and fold it in half, widthwise. Apply double-sided tape to the back of the white card stock invite and adhere it to the inside of the black card stock (photo B).

6. The next steps are all assembly, perfect for helpers of all skill levels. Place the piece of ribbon lengthwise on top of the patterned paper (photo C). Secure the ribbon by taping down the ends on the back of the yellow card stock.

7. Now tape the paper-punched picture of the super-cute bride-to-be to the front cover of the invite so that it overlaps the ribbon and patterned paper (photo D).

C.   D.

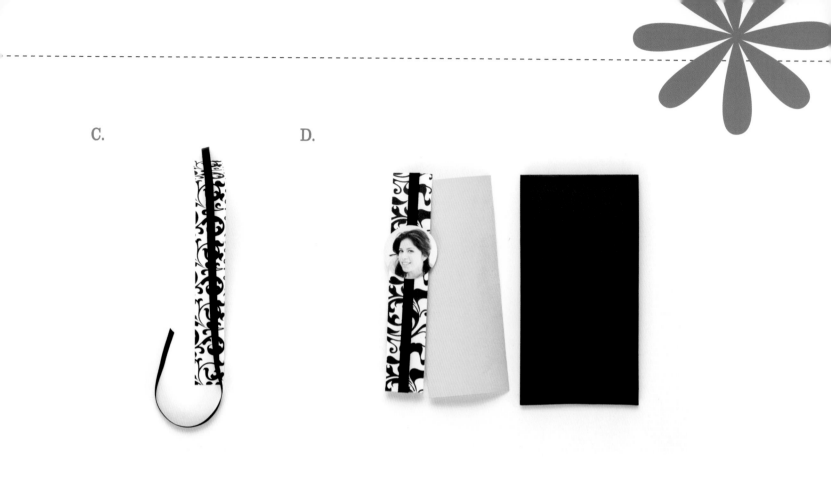

8. Take the piece of patterned paper and place it on top of the yellow card stock, aligned slightly to the right as shown in the photo on p. 110. You can also center the patterned paper on the yellow card stock for a more symmetrical look. Tape the patterned paper down to the back of the yellow card stock.

9. Finish it all up by attaching the three-layered paper you just created (yellow card stock, patterned paper, and ribbon) to the front of the black card stock (with the invitation on white card stock inside), off-center and to the right (or centered, depending on your preference), with double-sided tape.

tips & hints

- Remember, Microsoft Word is different for PCs and Macs, so if you're having problems, click on Help for assistance.

- These invitations require a special envelope size, 6^3/$_4$ in. by 3^1/$_2$ in. Websites like Action Envelope^{SM} and Stampin' Up!$^®$ are great sources for them.

- If the whole girly vibe isn't right for you, don't be afraid to play around with different colors and patterns of paper and ribbon. This project is simply a guide to jump-start your own creativity!

- While you may be tempted to use a black-and-white photo, do know that small black-and-white shots can look washed out against bold and bright colors.

- Camera shy? No problem! Substitute a monogram or logo or have a talented friend create a custom caricature of your pretty face.

Crafty Calculator

WHAT TO BUDGET

Paper and card stock	$ 15.00
Ribbon	$ 3.00
Paper punch	$ 8.00
Total (for 20 invites)	$26.00

COST COMPARISON

Custom bachelorette invitations from a stationer can cost upward of $2.50 per invitation. Our DIY version costs only $1.30.

STORE COST	YOUR COST
$2.50	$1.30

Months to go!

5

4

3

8

7

6

5

4

Weeks to go!

8-4 Weeks to Go!

SETTING THE SCENE FOR THE WEDDING

Yikes! Where'd the time go? As the days just fly by, it's time to start focusing on outfitting your ceremony and reception. There's nothing generic about you, Bride, so why should your ceremony or reception be anything but a reflection of your style sensibilities? The projects in this section focus on decor like funky beach glass hurricane centerpieces and sewn wedding programs that are sure to impress. Gather together your favorite dudes and dudettes and throw a crafting party complete with snacks and drinks. (Trust me on this: Few people can resist the lure of free food and beverage.) They get the opportunity to share in the great times leading to your special day, and you get to see your one-of-a-kind ceremony and reception come together before your very eyes!

This is a day for remembering
all the beautiful things
that have been
and a day for looking forward
to all the beautiful things
yet to come.

Love in Lights Wall Projection

You're not just a couple. You're a personal brand. You've put your custom logo on the invitations, programs, cocktail napkins, thank-you cards, favors—pretty much all the wedding accoutrements you can get your hands on. For oh-so-clever you, though, that's not enough. Where else or how else can you leave a personal mark on your wedding day? How about your venue's walls?

You can turn a blank wall into your own personal billboard of sorts. Showcase your personal monogram or logo. Display a favorite photo from your engagement session. Share your most beloved sonnet. All you need is a piece of paper with your chosen black-and-white artwork and a projector.

Time Wise

Depending on how much time you spend on the design, you can have this project completed in under 1 hour (or even less than 5 minutes if you're speedy!).

•

A Little Me Time

While you can complete the design on your own at home, be sure to hand off the projector and paper to a trusted friend or wedding coordinator for proper setup before the reception.

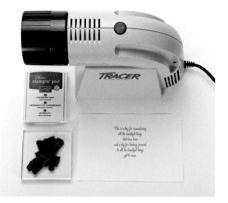

SUPPLIES

- Computer with Microsoft Word
- Printer
- White printer paper
- Art projector

For venues that won't allow you to pin or post anything on the walls, this is a great noninvasive solution for adding visual interest and mood-setting decor. It leaves no marks and can be set up in just minutes. Be warned, however, that it works best in a very dark area. Otherwise, the image will be washed out. A dark corner of your venue is your best bet for projecting the sign of your wedded bliss all evening (think near the gift table). Or save it for display behind the bride and groom's table when the lights go down for the first dance. Very dramatic!

DIRECTIONS

1. The hardest part of this project is creating the design of the image you want to project on the wall, so let's get started! The first thing you'll need to do is figure out how large your printed artwork needs to be. Read the manufacturer's recommendations on how much your art projector can enlarge an image (our projector's maximum was 14 times the original artwork's size) and the largest copy size it can handle (ours was 5 in. square). This establishes how large your artwork should be—you want the largest possible size that your machine will accommodate.

2. Open Microsoft Word and create a new document. Create a text box in the document. Double-click the edge of the text box and a Format text box will appear. Enter the dimensions of your artwork (5 in. by 5 in., for example). I'd recommend going with the largest copy size that your projector can handle. Click inside the text box and insert your artwork—personalized monogram or logo, clip art, photo, or favorite romantic quote. Get creative by mixing and matching these for a look you love! Just remember to stay in the parameters of the text box, so that nothing gets cut off once the artwork is projected on the walls. Save your document and then print it onto a regular piece of printer paper.

3. At the venue, plug in the art projector and insert the artwork on the glass projection screen. (See your projector's manual for exact instructions on how and where to position the artwork because each machine model is different.) Adjust the distance between the projector and wall to get the best image resolution. That's all there is to it!

tips & hints

- Remember, Microsoft Word is different for PCs and Macs, so if you're having problems, click on Help for assistance.

- We framed our wall projection by propping a large empty frame against the wall and projecting the artwork in the middle of it. It's not necessary, but it adds a fun touch. Scour secondhand stores and yard sales for deals on ornate frames.

- There are many models of projectors. Typically, the better projection, the higher the price. Be careful! Projectors can sometimes cost hundreds or thousands of dollars. Look for one at a hobby or craft store that enlarges type or artwork up to 14 times its original size.

- Keep an eye out for discount coupons from your local craft stores. A projector will cost about $80.00 retail, but you can score one at 40 percent to 50 percent off with a coupon.

- Black-and-white images project better than color.

- An image will be crisper in a low-light or dark area. Too much light, and the image may wash out or disappear completely.

- Another way to add extra oomph to your wall projection artwork is by decorating the paper with stamps after you print it out.

- Remember to pack an extra extension cord in case your venue doesn't have outlets near your setup area. Projector cords can be on the short side.

- Your art projector will come in handy for other crafty needs once your reception is over. They're great help when creating large paintings, banners, or murals or when you need to make a small image larger for tracing.

Crafty Calculator

WHAT TO BUDGET

Projector	$50.00
Paper & Printing	$ 0.50
Total	$50.50

COST COMPARISON

DJs and lighting companies can create custom wall projections called "gobos" that work with industrial lighting rigs. Expect to pay a minimum of $80.00 for just the custom gobo. Lighting rental will cost a lot—at least $250.00 extra. Your DIY version will cost only $50.50 if you buy the projector with a coupon, and you get to the keep the projector for other crafty projects.

STORE COST	YOUR COST
$330.00	**$50.50**

Karinna & Garrett

April 23, 2010

Prelude
  Mr. J.D. Alston

Entrance
  Groom's Father
  Bride's Mother
  Pastor
  Groom and Best Man

Processional of Bridal Party
  "Jesu, Joy of Man's Desire"

Bridal Introit
  "Trumpet Voluntary"

Invocation
  Bishop Walter S. Thomas Sr.

Scripture
  Ms. Michelle Hooper

Solo: "Finally I"
  Mr. Tyrone Wilson

Charge to the Couple

Exchange of Vows

Exchange of Rings

Blessing

Sew Divine Ceremony Program

The best weddings I've been to have made everyone attending feel as though they were an integral part of the celebration. A super-simple way to help guests get that warm, fuzzy feeling is to present them with a wedding program at your ceremony.

Programs introduce your wedding party, give an overview of the ceremony timelines, and help your guests understand the traditions you've incorporated into your unique event.

My problem with most programs is that they're boring. With a little bit of effort you can spruce up a basic program, and make it something special. Start off with an unusual paper size. Add a few pieces of punched paper. Finish it off with some stitching. Ta da!—high style and budget-friendly goodness in just minutes per program.

Time Wise

Once your programs are printed, you can expect to assemble and sew 5 to 10 of them in 1 hour.

A Little Me Time

This solo project is just the thing to get your weekend started right. Put on some high-octane tunes to keep the momentum going as you punch, sew, and assemble.

8

7

6

5

4

Weeks to go!

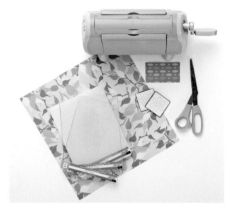

SUPPLIES

- Computer with Microsoft Word
- Printer
- Card stock, 6½ in. by 8½ in.
- Paper punches
- Cuttlebug machine
- Patterned scrapbook paper, 12 in. by 12 in.
- Hot glue gun and glue sticks
- Sewing machine and extra needles
- Cotton thread
- Scissors

A.

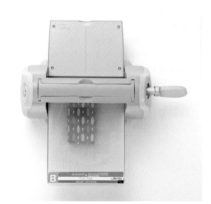

DIRECTIONS

1. The first step is to create the program in Microsoft Word. Go to File and choose Page Setup. From the Paper Size bar, scroll down and select Manage Custom Sizes. On the bottom of the dialog box that appears, click the + button and enter "6.5 x 8.5" into the field. This creates a custom page size. In the fields to the right side of the dialog box, enter "8.5" for the height and "6.5" for the width. Use "0.25" for the top, bottom, left, and right margins. Click OK. This will drop you back to the Page Setup menu. Click the Portrait orientation, and then click OK again. Now you've got a template for your program.

2. Because you'll be adding paper embellishments to the left side of the program, you'll want to print the program's text on the right side. To do this, create a text box on the right-hand side of the template. Adjust the size by clicking on one corner of the text box and dragging it with your mouse (aim for around 7 in. by 3½ in.). Click inside the text box and insert your program text. Save your document, and then print it on the card stock.

3. Once your programs are printed, the next step is to affix punched paper embellishments to the left-hand side of the program. Using paper punches or a die–cutting machine, punch out shapes from the patterned paper (photo A). Use the glue sick to apply to the back of the punch-outs, affix them to the program (photo B), and allow the glue to completely dry before moving on to the next step.

4. It's time to sew! Spend some time learning to how to thread your model, adjust the tension, and get it to work on your particular paper. I highly recommend doing a few test runs on scrap paper. Once you've got the hang of it, stitch from one end of the program to the other, alongside or over top the paper pieces you affixed to the left side of the program (photo C). If you're a newbie to sewing, go with a straight, freestyle stitch. Freestyle stitching is purposely carefree and imperfect and adds a fun look to your design.

5. Once the program is stitched, trim the excess threads with scissors, and you're done!

B.

C.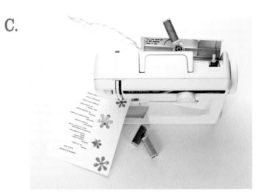

tips & hints

- *Remember, Microsoft Word is different for PCs and Macs, so if you're having problems, click on Help for assistance.*

- *Have extra sewing needles on hand. Needles can break, jam, or dull very easily when sewing on paper.*

- *Getting the right thread tension on your sewing machine is the most common problem for this project. If your tension is too tight, loops of the bobbin thread come up through the holes in the paper. Turn your tension dial to a lower number and try again.*

- *If your thread tension is too loose, you will see loose threads on the reverse side of your card stock.*

- *This can cause loose, bunched-up threads to seize up your machine. To correct this problem, increase the tension on your dial.*

- *Instead of patterned paper, you can use fabric for your embellishments. Either hand-cut the shapes or use a die-cutting machine to get the shapes you want.*

- *Paper punches can be layered on top of each other to create unique designs and add more texture to the program.*

- *Whenever possible go with a regular, standard-size sewing machine. The mini craft machines tend to be very poorly made and, in my experience, aren't worth buying.*

Crafty Calculator

WHAT TO BUDGET

Card stock	$25.00
Patterned paper	$10.00
Paper punch	$12.00
Thread	$ 3.00
Glue stick	$ 3.00
Total (for 100 programs)	$53.00

COST COMPARISON

Depending on what tools you already have, this DIY project will cost just a little more than $0.50 per program. Custom sewn programs from a stationer will often run $8.00 or more.

STORE COST	YOUR COST
$8.00	**53¢**

Weeks to go!

8
7
6
5
4

Glitter & Shine Monogram

Oh, glitter, how I adore your sparkly blinged-out goodness. Is there anything you can't make better? I submit there is not! Take this door monogram, for example. What started off as a homely sheet of white craft foam is miraculously transformed into a glamorous adornment that'll greet your guests at the ceremony door. Who wouldn't feel like a VIP when gliding through an entrance topped with this?

For just a few dollars and a few minutes of your time, you can create this chic glittery monogram at home. There are dozens of gorgeous hues of glitter on the market to match your decor and preferred level of glitterification. But beware: Glitter is highly addictive! Once you get a taste for it, be prepared to start looking for ways to add a bit of the "Big G" to all of your crafting projects.

Time Wise

Allow yourself 1 hour or so for this project. While it's easy to do, sculpting the foam will take some time. It's best to allow the adhesive to dry overnight before you display your glittery creation.

A Little Me Time

Parts of this super-easy solo project should be done outdoors, but spend the remainder of your crafty time listening to tunes or catching up on your favorite TV shows.

8

7

6

5

4

Weeks to go!

SUPPLIES

- Computer and printer
- 1-in.-thick craft foam, at least 15 in. by 15 in.
- Permanent marker
- Craft knife or serrated knife
- Ruler or straightedge
- Sandpaper or heavy-duty emery board
- Newspaper to protect your work surface
- Foam brush
- White craft glue
- Glitter
- Craft wire, about 18 in.
- Wire cutters

A.

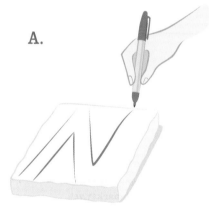

B.

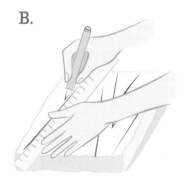

DIRECTIONS

1. Before you get started, you'll need to decide on your monogram design. Once you decide on a font style, print out your initial(s) in the largest size you can to see if you like the look of the monogram and if it'll work when carved in foam. Fonts with thin lines or a lot of curves will be difficult to cut from the foam. Try to stay with bold lines.

2. The next step is to draw the letter on the face of the foam with a permanent marker (drawing A). If you're not good with freehand drawing, an alternative is to have an enlarged print of the initial made at a copy shop. This'll cost anywhere from a few cents to a few dollars, depending on the size of the paper and the shop. Trace the printout onto the foam sheet by taping it to the foam and pressing over the lines of the letter with a hard object like the tip of a pencil or even a screwdriver.

3. Now that you've got your initial transferred onto the foam, it's time to cut it out with the craft or serrated knife, using a ruler to give you a nice straight edge to cut along (drawing B). I recommend doing this outside because foam dust and bits will get everywhere. Take your time with this step! Foam is brittle and breaks easily. Once your initial is carved from the foam, smooth out the edges of the letter with a piece of sandpaper or a heavy-duty emery board.

4. It's time to glue. Place newspaper on your work surface to protect it before starting this step. Using a foam brush, apply a generous, even coat of craft glue to the front and sides of the initial (drawing C). You don't need to cover the back of the letter unless your guests will be able to see it.

5. Are you ready to get your glitter on? Working quickly before the glue begins to dry, pour glitter all over the sticky glued surface of the initial (drawing D). Don't hold back! The thicker the layer of glitter, the better the coverage will be. Use your fingers to press and smooth the glitter onto the surface of the initial. If you find areas on the monogram with uneven glitter coverage, add a bit of glue to those spots and—that's right!—pour on more glitter.

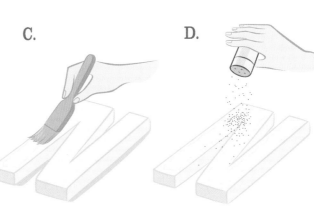

C.

D.

6. Gently shake off any excess glitter onto a sheet of newspaper. Again, it's best to do this outside. Glitter will get everywhere, and it is a pain to clean up. Allow your glittered initial to dry overnight or per the glue manufacturer's recommended drying time.

7. The last step is to create a wire hanger to attach the monogram to the church or venue door. Cut a length of wire, about 18 in. long. Insert each end of the wire through the sides of the initial and out the back, about 1 in. from the top of the foam initial. Twist the ends together to close the loop and you'll be good to go when it's time to hang the monogram. If your venue does not allow you to hang anything on doors or walls (be sure to ask ahead of time), this project looks great displayed on the cake table, the bride and groom's table, a mantel, or windowsill.

tips & hints

- There are different grades of glitter: ultra-fine, fine, medium, and chunky. Typically, the larger the glitter particle, the more shine and bling factor it has.

- Most glitter is made of plastic-type materials. Glass glitter (or German glass glitter) does exist and is made of, you guessed it, crushed glass. This is consider-ably more expensive than regular glitter but has an amazing sparkle. Do be extra careful if you decide to use glass glitter—it will cut you and embed its tiny particles in your skin if you don't wear gloves. Ouch!

- Consider doing a few letters—maybe the first initials of you and your guy or, if you're not taking your hubby's last name, both of your last initials.

Crafty Calculator

WHAT TO BUDGET

Sheet of craft foam	$8.00
Glue	$3.00
Glitter, 5 oz.	$8.00
Wire	$3.00
Total	$22.00

COST COMPARISON

I haven't seen anything like this available on the bridal market yet. Door monograms made of fresh flowers will cost $40.00 or more. So in addition to being a trendsetter, you get a gorgeous monogram at almost half the price!

STORE COST	YOUR COST
$40.00	**$22.00**

Beach Glass Centerpiece

The e-mail starts, like so many others in my inbox, like this:

DIY Bride,

We're having a small wedding reception on the beach next summer. Our goal is to create an elegant, intimate setting using candles and beach-like materials. The problem? We have nearly no budget and need something for less than $20.00 each. Local florists laugh at us when we mention our budget and we're 100 percent overwhelmed at the craft stores. Help!

Signed,

Trish & Tom Tormented

Time Wise

If you tackle this project with a team, you can complete 5 to 8 vases in 1 hour.

Divide & Conquer

Would any of your girls turn down daiquiris and delicious food? I didn't think so! Bring out the blender and the berries, have your hubby-to-be throw some sliders on the grill, and set up stations to keep the craft moving.

SUPPLIES

- Clear glass cylinder vase
- Glass cleaner
- Paper towels
- White wax pencil
- Hot glue gun and glue sticks
- Sea (beach) glass

My reply:

Dear Tormented Micro-Budget Bride and Groom,

Your plea for an elegant centerpiece project that's inexpensive and easy has been heard. I bring you the beach glass vase, an under-$20.00 project that's perfect for bringing on the casual beach elegance vibe to your table decor. Filled with sand, shells, and a pillar candle or with water and a floating candle, these centerpieces are sure to add warmth and style to your reception. The best part is that nearly anyone, regardless of previous crafting experience, can create these with supplies found at most craft stores.

DIRECTIONS

1. Clean the outside of the vase with glass cleaner and a paper towel. Let them completely air dry. This removes any dirt, oils, or other debris from the surface of the vase so that the sea glass will better adhere to it.

2. Draw guidelines for the glass pieces on the outside of the vase with the wax pencil (drawing A). If you want to redraw any lines, just use glass cleaner to wipe off the wax marks and redraw them until you are satisfied with your pattern.

STATION 1: VASE CLEANING
Put a pair of ladies to work getting the vases squeaky clean for crafting.

STATION 2: PENCILING
Get your girls with an eye for design to pencil patterns on the vases.

STATION 3: GLUE AND GLASS
Put your steadiest hands (and the ones that don't mind getting a little sticky!) to work at this station, putting sea glass on the vases with hot glue.

STATION 4: POLISHING
Put a couple of girls in charge of shining the vases with glass cleaner.

A.

B.

3. Apply a small bead of hot glue directly to the surface of the vase, on top of the wax pencil guideline, and press a piece of sea glass in place (drawing B). Hold it there for a few seconds. Repeat with additional pieces of glass until you have traced out your entire penciled-in pattern.

4. If you spot any residue or fingerprints, bring out the glass cleaner and polish up your finished product, inside the vase and carefully around the sea glass.

tips & hints

- If you can't find a white wax pencil, go with the lightest color you can find. That way, the wax guidelines won't be easily seen when the vases are put on display.

- Any size or shape of glass vase can work for this project, but you'll want one with a solid surface so the sea glass will stick.

- Sea glass comes in a variety of colors including white, blue, green, gray, and black. It can be found at well-stocked craft stores and online.

- You don't have to limit yourself to a random arrangement of sea glass! Gorgeous geometrics, table numbers, and monograms can be made out of the sea glass, too.

- The best deals for sand can be found by buying in bulk from home and garden stores. Look for bags of "play sand" in the garden department.

Crafty Calculator

WHAT TO BUDGET

10-in. glass vase	$10.00
Sea glass, ½ lb.	$ 2.50
Glue sticks	$ 5.00
Total	$17.50

COST COMPARISON

Decorated vases can cost upward of $40.00 each at boutiques. Our version costs about $17.50, not including a candle.

STORE COST	YOUR COST
$40.00	**$17.50**

Groovy Owl Cake Topper

I have had a serious thing about owls lately. It may be nostalgia from my 1970s earth-toned home decor upbringing or it could be because owls are just so cute in a kitschy way. Combine my weakness for all things vintage with my love for outdoorsy-themed weddings, and this fondant owl topper is my idea of retro heaven on a cake platter. Adorable, whimsical, unique, and pretty darned easy to make—could this great little gem of a topper make you fall in love, too?

No special skills are needed for this project, which was inspired by a cake made by chef Duff Goldman on his popular Food Network® show, *Ace of Cakes*, and the supplies can be found in the baking aisle of most craft stores. Specialty cake supply shops will also have the necessary ingredients and will, most likely, have a wider selection of fondant brands and colorants.

Time Wise

A team of three should finish these toppers in 2 to 3 hours.

•

It's a Girl Thing

This is an ambitious craft, but with the right company, you'll fly through it. Work with a couple of your best girls, preferably a pair that is not sugar-averse. Set aside an afternoon and gather your flock, and be sure to fuel the fun with a tray of cute cupcakes and bubbly champagne!

SUPPLIES

- Ready-to-use white fondant, 32 oz. (2 lb.)
- Powdered sugar
- Latex gloves
- Waxed paper
- Gel food color in brown, orange, yellow, and green
- Toothpicks
- 18-gauge to 20-gauge wire, about 10 in.
- Wire cutters
- Groovy Owl Cake Topper Templates, at right
- Rolling pin
- Craft knife or sharp kitchen knife
- Small foam brush
- Small container of water
- Bamboo skewers

While the fondant owls are edible, I wouldn't recommend eating them after they've been displayed at the wedding. The potential sugar coma alone might be enough to make you shy away.

DIRECTIONS

1. Your first task is to "condition" the fondant (that's fancy chef-speak). When you pull it from the package, you'll notice it's a solid lump—not very conducive to molding and shaping. Conditioning simply means you're going to knead the fondant until it becomes pliable dough, just like you would with bread or clay. Put the lump of fondant in the microwave on high for 10 seconds to 15 seconds. Dust your work surface with powdered sugar, then place your softened fondant in the center. Use the heel of your hands to compress and push the fondant away from you, then fold it back over itself. Keep folding over and compressing the fondant until it becomes smooth and easy to shape. This will take about 5 minutes.

2. Use one-third of the fondant to make 1 large lump. Then form three equal-size lumps from the remaining fondant, and set two of these aside. Take the third lump and divide it into two equal-size pieces. The large lump will be for your owls' bodies, wings, noses, eyelashes, and pupils. The two medium lumps will be for the owls' white and orange feathers, and the two small lumps will be for the yellow feathers and green eyes, and the male owl's dapper green bow tie.

3. Put on those latex gloves, cover your work surface with waxed paper, and let's color the fondant! Gel coloring will stain your hands—and anything else it comes in contact with, so do wear gloves and an apron or clothes you won't mind getting stained. Here's the plan: You'll be coloring the large fondant lump brown. Leave one medium lump white, and the other should be colored orange. One of the small lumps should be yellow and the other, green. For each color, dip a clean toothpick into one of the pots of gel coloring and wipe it on the surface of the corresponding fondant ball. Work the color into each fondant by kneading it as you did in Step 1. Remember to wash your gloves

off after working in each color to prevent cross-staining. If you put the lumps of fondant in the microwave to soften them, be sure to zap them for only 5 seconds at a time, and don't use the microwave until you've mixed the color in thoroughly. Add more color as needed to achieve the look you are going for. Add a little color at a time because it's easier to build up color to make it richer than to try to lighten it.

Groovy Owl Cake Topper Templates

Trace or reproduce these templates for your cake toppers.

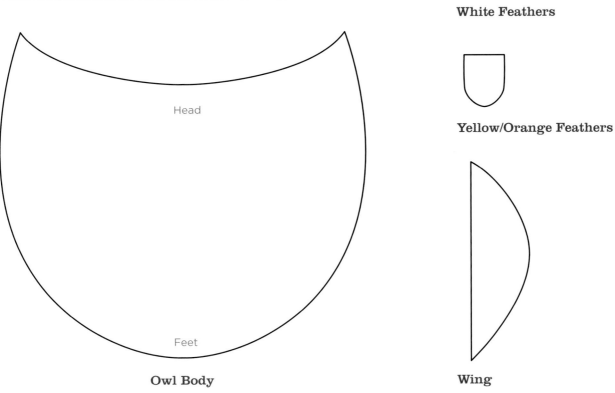

Head

Feet

Owl Body

White Feathers

Yellow/Orange Feathers

Wing

A.

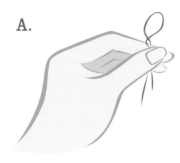

B.

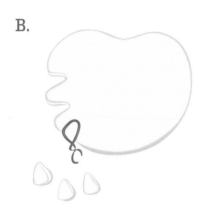

C.

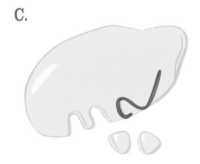

4. Let's make body parts! Make sure your gloves are clean, and then pull a golf ball–size piece of fondant from the brown lump and set it aside. Divide the remaining brown fondant into two equal-size portions for two owl bodies. Using the body template (p. 137), form the basic owl shape. Each owl should be at least 1½ in. thick to provide stability. Set aside.

5. Next, you'll make feather punchers out of wire. Think of these tools as mini cookie cutters (with a handle) for the owls' feathers. Cut the 10-in. length of wire in half, and shape one piece of wire like the white feather template (p. 137) and the other like the yellow/orange feather template (p. 137). Use the tail end of the wire as a handle (drawing A).

6. On a surface dusted with powdered sugar, roll out the white fondant to a ¹⁄₁₆-in. thickness. Using the white feather punch, work around the edges of your rolled-out fondant and cut out 60 white feathers (drawing B). Don't worry if the edges of your feathers aren't perfectly smooth. Later, when you attach them to the owls' bodies, the water you use as an adhesive will smooth out any imperfections. Set your white feathers aside.

7. Powder your work surface with more powdered sugar, then roll out the orange and yellow fondant to a ¹⁄₁₆-in. thickness. Using the yellow/orange feather puncher, cut out 80 orange feathers and 25 yellow feathers (drawing C). Set them aside. You're almost done. Hang in there!

8. Next, wipe down your work surface and roll out your golf ball–size piece of brown fondant to a ⅛-in. thickness on a surface dusted with powdered sugar. Use the white feather puncher to cut out two pieces. These will be the noses for your owls! Then place the wing template (p. 137) on the rolled-out brown fondant and cut around it with a craft knife or small, sharp kitchen knife. You'll need four wings. Set these pieces aside.

9. It's time to create the last details. Use scraps of white fondant to create four small circles for the base of your owls' eyes. An easy way to do this is to roll the scrap of fondant into a little ball (about the size of a popcorn kernel) and then flatten it. Do the same with green fondant, creating four flat discs that are a bit smaller than the white ones you just made. Then use leftover brown fondant to create four tiny pupils.

10. Roll thin scraps of brown fondant between your thumb and forefingers to create the female owl's eyelashes, three for each eye (see photo on p. 134). Set these pieces aside. Use green fondant scraps to form the male owl's bow tie. A simple way to do this is to roll out the green fondant on a surface dusted with powdered sugar, cut out an oval-shaped piece about $1\frac{1}{2}$ in. long and $\frac{1}{2}$ in. wide, and pinch it in the center. Then, roll a small piece of green fondant (about the size of a popcorn kernel) into a ball and flatten it as you did when creating the eyes in Step 9. Use this piece for the knot at the center of the tie, covering the pinched area.

11. Now, the fun part: assembly! Keep in mind that we are decorating the fronts of each owl. Don't wrap the feathers around the back or you'll need a lot more fondant! Use a foam brush to apply water to the fondant throughout the assembly process to keep the surface tacky, so that the fondant pieces stick to each other. But each time you moisten your brush, wring out any excess water so you don't have a sticky mess. If the excessive water dissolves too much fondant, the colors will bleed. This is particularly problematic when it comes to working with and around the white feathers, so be careful!

    First, attach the white feathers. You will use 20 to 30 white feathers for each owl. Using your foam brush, moisten the bottom half of each owl's body. Attach the white feathers to the owl body in straight rows, working from the feet of the owl upward, overlapping each row of

D.

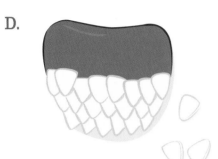

feathers for a layered effect (drawing D). Try for three complete rows of white feathers. It is helpful to moisten the back of each feather before attaching it; this creates a surface with extra sticking force and smooths out imperfections. If you run out of feathers, simply roll out scraps of white fondant and punch more.

12. Next, let's give your owls some eyes! With your foam brush, moisten the upper half of the owl bodies as well as the top row of white feathers, where the orange eye feathers will overlap. Attach the orange, and then the yellow, feathers in three nested circles, with each inner circle getting smaller and tighter (drawing E). Each eye will need about 20 orange feathers and 6 yellow feathers. Start with an outer circle made of overlapping orange feathers. The feathers at the bottom of the circle should slightly overlap the top row of white feathers. Continuing with the orange feathers, make a smaller circle inside the outer circle. Use yellow feathers for the final, smallest circle. Again, moistening the backs of the feathers will ensure that they stick and will smooth out imperfections. If you run out of feathers, simply roll out orange or yellow fondant scraps and punch out more.

E.

13. When your nested feather circles for the eyes are complete, it is time to place your owls' eyes inside! Using the foam brush, moisten the backs of the white fondant pieces and place one in the center of each yellow circle. Then, moisten the green circles and place one in the center of each white circle. Finally, attach the pupils to the green circles. Apply a bit of pressure to secure them.

F.

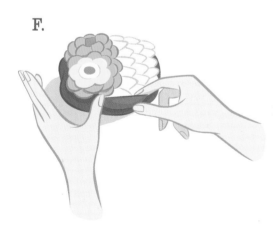

14. Now it's time to attach the final details! Moisten the back of each owl's nose and place it between the owl's eyes, so that the bottom of the nose lines up with the base of the outermost circle of orange feathers. The pointy tip of the nose faces up (the opposite of the way you put the white feathers on). Moisten the back of each wing and attach them to the sides of the owl (drawing F). The wings should be just visible when facing the owls head on, and will barely overlap the owl's white feathers. Finally, moisten and place the female's eyelashes and the male's bow tie as you see fit. Voilà! Aren't they adorable?

15. The last step is to insert a bamboo skewer into the bottom of each owl. This provides stability and a way for cake toppers to sit securely on top of the wedding cake. But make sure not to push the skewers too deep. You don't want them popping through your owls' heads.

tips & hints

- *If at any time you feel that your owl's appearance would benefit from the placement of additional feathers, it's fairly simple to attach them. Use a toothpick to gently lift feathers that might be in the way and carefully slide additional feathers into place.*

- *I chose to add a veil made of tulle and attached it with a pushpin to my female owl, but let your own style shine through! Also, don't be limited by my suggested colors. Gel food color come in a rainbow of shades. Customize your owls any way you'd like.*

- *The owls can be made up to 2 months in advance, but must be kept tightly sealed in a good-quality plastic food container, lined with waxed or parchment paper, and refrigerated until use.*

Let your owls dry overnight before storing them so they don't stick to the waxed paper.

- *Colored fondant will fade in direct sunlight, but it should be fine on display for a few hours.*

- *Unfortunately, fondant is not made for long-term preservation. Though I've heard of instances in which people have been able to save their fondant designs for posterity by putting shellac or resin on them, I'm doubtful that'd work for this project. Consider your owls to be disposable goods.*

Crafty Calculator

WHAT TO BUDGET

Fondant	$15.00
Food color	$ 8.00
Gloves	$ 1.00
Wire	$ 4.00
Bamboo skewers	$ 3.00
Total	$31.00

COST COMPARISON

Edible custom cake toppers are sometimes included in the price of a wedding cake, but many customized toppers can cost over $100.00. Our pretty pair is considerably less and can be customized any way you'd like.

STORE COST	YOUR COST
$100.00	**$31.00**

8
7
6
5
4

Weeks to go!

3-1 Week to Go!

CRAFTING A ONE-OF-A-KIND RECEPTION

It's crunch time! The final few weeks before your wedding will likely be super-crazy, but the projects in this section are sure stress-relievers because they'll get you focused on the free-flowing fun of your reception. Set aside some alone time to get the seating chart for the reception in order and to stamp your gorgeous custom cocktail napkins. Then, take a stroll down memory lane and craft your table markers. You're creating the final details for the ceremony and reception with custom-made decor and accessories during these weeks, and checking them off your list will put your busy mind at ease. Exactly what every bride needs!

Justamere Lane

This is the street where Elizabeth grew up, and where her parents reside to this day. Mom's baking and Dad's grilling entice countless guests each year; her childhood home on Justamere Lane will always be one of Elizabeth's favorite places.

Memory Lane Table Marker

When I was in the midst of planning my wedding and addressing invitations to family and old friends, I couldn't help but reminisce. In my mind I walked, with my loved ones, through the town I grew up in, the lake I visit ever year with my family, the places I traveled after graduating college. Enter my now-husband and a new set of special places. In retrospect, I realize that there's a great way to honor such memories—share them with your wedding guests!

Get together with your hubby-to-be and brainstorm a list of your favorite places. The streets you both grew up on, the café where you met, your favorite vacation spot—all of these would make excellent table names! Accent the cards with a corner hole punch in a cute design—oodles are available at most craft stores—and ribbon to fit your theme.

Time Wise

Once you've printed your card stock, you can complete 10 to 15 of these super-simple table names in 1 hour.

A Little Me Time

This is a perfect project to tackle during downtime. Creating your template takes focus, but you can punch corners while you jam out to a pre-wedding playlist, cut and tie the ribbons in front of your fave prime-time TV show, and glue the bows to the printed cards while you catch up with a friend on speakerphone!

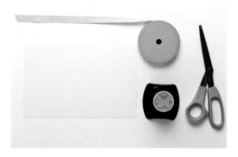

SUPPLIES

- Computer with Microsoft Word
- Printer
- Card stock, 4½ in. by 5½ in.
- Corner punch
- Ribbon, 8 in. to 10 in.
- Scissors
- Hot glue gun and glue sticks

DIRECTIONS

1. Create your table marker template by opening a new Word document and going to File menu and choose Page Setup. From the Paper Size bar, scroll down and select Manage Custom Sizes. On the bottom of the dialog box that appears, click the + button and enter "4.25 x 5.5" into this field. This creates a custom page size. In the fields to the right side of the dialog box, enter "4.25" for the height and "5.5" for the width. Use "0.75" for the top margin and "0.25" for the bottom, left, and right margins. The extra margin space on top leaves room for your bow! Click OK. This will drop you back to the Page Setup menu. Click the Landscape orientation, and then hit OK again.

2. Add the table names to the cards by selecting a font size, style, and color for the table card, and click the Align Center button in the MS Word toolbar. Type the name of your first favorite place. Choose a fairly large font size for this so that your guests can easily identify the table names.

3. Next, select a font style, color, and size for the description of your favorite locale that will go under the place name. Hit Enter one or two times and insert the description. Try to limit yourself to two or three sentences per place.

4. Save each table card separately according to the name of the table. That way if you want to change a few lines here and there later on, you can. Now print the table names on the card stock—you'll do this twice per card, so that the table marker is double-sided. Let the ink dry after the first printing. Then, feed the card stock back into the printer and print on the reverse side. Repeat Steps 2–4 for each unique table name and description. You may want to change up the font style and color on the cards by table or go with a consistent look—you decide!

5. Bring out your corner punch and find a hard, steady surface like a table or countertop. Play around with scrap paper before punching your completed cards. Perhaps you want just the tip of each corner of the card to be embellished, or maybe you want a full inch or two decorated. Insert one corner of your printed card stock into the corner punch and press down

firmly—remember, card stock is thicker than regular paper. Punch all four corners of each table name in this manner (photo A).

6. Cut your ribbon in half to get two 4- to 5-in. lengths. Tie each piece of ribbon into a bow. You now have a bow for both sides of the table marker. Apply a teeny drop of hot glue to the back of one bow's knot and press the bow onto the card stock at the top of the card above the printed table name. Make sure that the tails of your bow don't cover the printed name; if they do, snip them with scissors until the view is unobstructed. Repeat with the second bow on the other side of the card stock. Do this for each table name, and then sit back to admire your adorably adorned Memory Lane Table Markers.

tips & hints

- *Remember, Microsoft Word is different for PCs and Macs, so if you're having problems, click on Help for assistance.*

- *If you don't dig bows, punch several holes along the top of the card stock and weave your ribbon through to create a lovely decorative border.*

- *You can choose any color card stock for your table markers. Just be sure that the font color contrasts well with the card stock.*

- *Use a corner punch to customize programs, menus, or thank-you cards—if it's a flat piece of paper with right-angle corners you can pull off the punch!*

- *Craft, party supply, and stationery stores often have neat table number display stands. Check the wedding-related aisles, too.*

- *For simple—and cheap—display stands, hit up your local restaurant supply stores. Even better? Ask your venue or your caterer if they have stands.*

- *If you can't find the right display stands, consider propping the cards up against your centerpieces.*

A.

Justamere Lane

This is the street where Elizabeth grew up, and where her parents reside to this day. Mom's baking and Dad's grilling entice countless guests each year; her childhood home on Justamere Lane will always be one of Elizabeth's favorite places.

Crafty Calculator

WHAT TO BUDGET

Corner punch	$10.00
Ribbon (3 yd.)	$ 3.00
Card stock	$ 5.00
Total (for 10 table markers)	$18.00

COST COMPARISON

Custom table markers can set you back upward of $3.00 each, and I guarantee they won't be crafted with the TLC that this project delivers. Your super-special DIY table markers are an absolute steal at around half the cost, and they personalize your wedding in a way that is (dare I say it?) priceless!

STORE COST	YOUR COST
$3.00	**$1.80**

Stamped Cocktail Napkin

Y ou, dear Bride and Groom, are the Queen and King of Small Details. While some may say you have control issues, you're secure in your love of luxurious frills.

Take the cocktail napkin. A necessity, yes, but . . . ugh! Could it be any more boring? Oh sure, there are preprinted paper napkins that are fine if you have a deep attachment to ghastly floral prints or cartoon characters. But for those of you with Cristal® tastes on a Samuel Adams® budget, novelty prints just aren't going to pass muster.

With a few supplies and steady hands, this project will show you how to turn boring old paper napkins into lovely pieces of cocktail hour couture for less than $0.20 each.

Time Wise

Depending on your stamping skills, you should be able to complete at least 24 napkins in less than 1 hour.

A Little Me Time

Recharge after a long day of work with some stamping action. Put on your favorite tunes and get your craft on.

SUPPLIES

- Scrap paper
- Paper cocktail napkins, found at any party supply store
- Rubber stamps
- Pigment ink pad
- Stamp cleaning pad and cleaning solution
- Ruler

DIRECTIONS

1. The first thing you'll need to do is protect your work surface. Pigment inks are permanent and will stain *everything* they touch. Cover your work area with scrap paper.

2. Place one cocktail napkin on your work surface.

3. Gently tap your stamp on the surface of the ink pad to ink it up. Tapping will help disperse ink evenly over the stamp surface. Too much ink will create smudges or pools of ink on the napkin.

4. Press the inked stamp firmly on the napkin to create the impression, and then lift the stamp straight up (photo A). Don't rock the stamp back and forth— that will cause smudges. Try a few practice runs on scrap paper to get the hang of how much ink and pressure to apply.

5. Set the napkin aside to dry for a minute or so. That's all there is to this project!

6. After each napkin, re-ink your stamp to get the best impressions.

7. When you're done stamping, clean your stamp by spritzing cleaner onto the stamp cleaning pad and then rubbing the stamp on the wet pad.

A.

B.

tips & hints

- It is important to use only pigment inks. They won't bleed or smudge on your guests' fingers or faces when the napkin is used.

- If you need to center your stamp on the napkin, a ruler like the one I used to position the 'T' stamp will come in handy (photo B).

- For cocktail hour, you'll need three to four napkins per guest.

- Custom rubber stamps can be made at office supply stores and purchased through online retailers.

- Pigment inks come in hundreds of colors—including white and metallic hues.

Crafty Calculator

WHAT TO BUDGET

Stamps	$15.00
Ink	$ 8.00
Napkins	$10.00
Total (for 200 napkins)	$33.00

COST COMPARISON

Specialty bridal retailers charge $50.00 or more for 200 custom cocktail napkins with limited design options. Our version comes to $33.00 for 200 napkins and can be customized any way you desire.

STORE COST	YOUR COST
$50.00	**$33.00**

Magnetic Clothespin Seating Chart

Bravo! You've finally found the perfect seat mate for crazy Aunt Edna. Your fiancé's mom is sitting nowhere near his dad and new wife. Those friends of the family that you see only at weddings are all well situated among guests with similar interests and backgrounds. You are the master of the diplomatic seating arrangement. Pat yourself on the back! That was no easy task.

Your next dilemma is how to display the seating assignments without locking yourself into a single, large design. You just know cousin Ted is about to break up with his girlfriend or that at any moment your co-worker will call to say that she's bringing her brand new boyfriend, and you'll have to scramble to make last-minute seating changes.

Time Wise

This project is easy to assemble, but allow yourself plenty of time for the paint to dry on the metal sheet. Expect 1 hour of drying time between coats plus about 10 minutes of work for each of the seating chart cards.

A Little Me Time

Once you and your fiancé have decided where to seat everyone, this is a great lazy-afternoon project. You'll be spray-painting the metal sheet, so throw on your sweats in case things get messy!

SUPPLIES

- 1 sheet of galvanized aluminum flashing, 24 in. by 36 in., available at hardware stores
- Spray paint in your choice of color
- Computer with Microsoft Word
- Printer
- Plain card stock, 4½ in. by 6½ in.
- Decorative card stock, 5 in. by 7 in.
- Double-sided tape
- Wooden clothespins, spring loaded
- Decorative paper, 12 in. by 12 in.
- Scissors or paper cutter
- Liquid craft glue
- Small magnets
- Ribbon

My simple solution is for you to create a magnetic seating chart with individual cards for each table. If anything needs to change at a table or if you need to add more tables, all you have to do is create or modify one of the cards. Even better? This seating chart has a clean modern look that you can accessorize with ribbon trim—a perfect way to incorporate your wedding colors and theme into the project.

DIRECTIONS

1. This project starts with a trip outside. In a well-ventilated space, spray a light, even coat of paint on the front of the aluminum flashing. Allow it to dry according to the manufacturer's instructions. Repeat 1 to 2 more times, until you get full, even coverage. Remember to allow the paint to dry between coats.

2. Next up: the seating chart cards, which will display a list of guests for each table. Open Microsoft Word and go to File menu and choose Page Setup. From the Paper Size bar, scroll down and select Manage Custom Sizes. On the bottom of the dialog box that appears, click the + button and enter "4.5 x 6.5" into this field. This creates a custom page size. In the fields to the right side of the dialog box, enter "6.5" for the height and "4.5" for the width. Use "0.25" for the top, bottom, left, and right margins. Click OK. This will drop you back to the Page Setup menu. Click the Portrait orientation, and then click OK again. You have the template for your table cards.

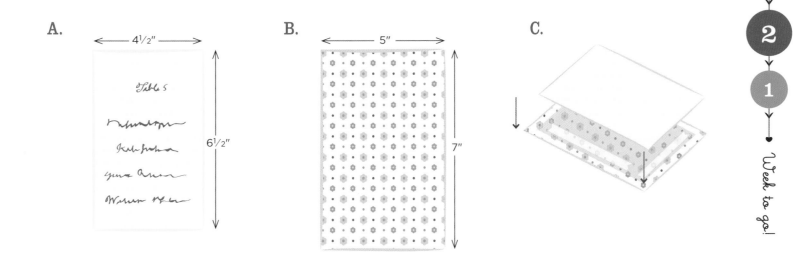

A.

← 4¹/₂" →

Table 5

6¹/₂"

B.

← 5" →

7"

C.

3. Now it's time to insert your table names or numbers along with the names of the guests at the table. Create a separate document for each table; I suggest saving each by table number. Print each list onto a piece of 4¹/₂-in. by 6¹/₂-in. card stock (drawing A).

4. The next step is to adhere the table cards to the 5-in. by 7-in. decorative card stock (drawing B). Apply double-sided tape to the back of the printed table cards, and mount each one onto a piece of the decorative card stock (drawing C). Be careful to center the printed card stock on the slightly larger decorative paper so that there's a border of pattern on all four sides.

D.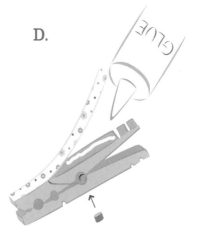

5. You're almost done! The next step is to decorate the clothespins and attach the magnets. Because there's no standard clothespin size, you'll need to measure the front of your clothespins and cut strips of decorative paper to those measurements. Apply a thin, even coat of liquid craft glue to the front of the clothespin and place the paper strips, pressing down to make sure they stick (drawing D). Let them dry for a few hours before the next step. To get the clothespins to stick to the painted metal board, use liquid craft glue to glue small magnets to the center of the back of the clothespins (drawing D). Allow the glue to dry for a few hours.

6. As a finishing touch, add a border of ribbon to the top, bottom, and sides of the board, securing the ribbon to the back of the board with double-sided tape. When you're ready to display the board, simply place a seating card in the jaws of the clothespin and stick it to the magnetic board.

tips & hints

- Remember, Microsoft Word is different for PCs and Macs, so if you're having problems, click on Help for assistance.

- Be extra careful when handling the metal sheet. The edges can sometimes be a little sharp.

- Most spray paints will work for this project, even though there are brands especially made for metal. Regular spray paints come in a large variety colors and are generally cheaper.

- After the wedding, the board can be used in your office to hold memos or photos. It's a neat keepsake!

- Look for "super" magnets at your local craft and hardware stores. They're a little more expensive than normal magnets, but they are stronger and will have a more secure grip on the metal board.

- The metal board can be a bit flimsy or wobbly. Setting it on an easel or against a wall is your best bet for keeping it upright.

- Make sure the font on your table cards is large enough and legible enough for your guests to see at a glance. Simple fonts are better than overly ornate ones, but don't be afraid to experiment with different styles.

Crafty Calculator

WHAT TO BUDGET

Aluminum flashing	$ 8.00
Spray paint	$ 5.00
Clothespins	$ 1.00
Card stock	$ 3.00
Magnets	$ 3.00
Total	$20.00

COST COMPARISON

Custom-designed seating charts from stationers and seating chart designers can cost upward of $125.00 or more. This DIY version costs $20.00. How sweet is that?

STORE COST	YOUR COST
$125.00	**$20.00**

Grace & Alan

Just Married

June 27, 2010

Just-Married Banner

Your wedding will be the epitome of style and perfection. The beautiful reception will be talked about in hushed, reverent tones for years to come. All great things must come to an end, of course, but you just cannot bear the idea of hopping into a sleek getaway car with tacky tin cans or silly streamers tied to the bumper.

The only stylish remedy is to create a stunning do-it-yourself just-married sign to let all passersby know that, yes, there's a fabulous newlywed couple in their midst.

This project is an easy one for crafty and non-crafty types alike. Most of it is done on your home computer, and then you drop by your local copy shop and have them create the finished product.

Time Wise

Once you get the completed poster back from the copy shop, this project will take about 2 hours to complete.

A Little Me Time

The finishing touches for this project are super-simple, so you'll have no problem completing it on your own.

SUPPLIES

- Computer with Microsoft Word
- CD drive and burner
- Spray adhesive
- Foam board
- Crop-A-Dile hole punch and eyelet setter tool
- Ribbon, at least 4 yd.
- Scissors

DIRECTIONS

1. Open Microsoft Word and create a new document. Go to File and choose Page Setup. Click on Landscape orientation.

2. Create a text box in the middle of the page, leaving a 1-in. margin around each side of the text box. You can adjust the size of the text box any time by clicking on a corner and dragging it with your mouse. Next, format the text box. Double click on the edge of the text box to get the Format menu. You'll have the option of inserting specific text box dimensions, background colors, border styles, and line types. For this example, we used a background color of periwinkle with no border or line styles.

3. It's time to add your text and any graphics to your just-married banner. Have fun with this step! Play around with font types and styles to create your own unique imprint. Print-quality graphics (300 dpi) may be used in this area, too.

4. When you're satisfied with the look, save your document and burn it to a CD. Remember to include copies of the fonts and graphics you've used so that when the file is opened on another computer, all the fonts and art will be there, too! Better yet, convert the Word file to a PDF file if your computer is set up to do so. Take the CD to a local copy shop and have it printed in color on a 16-in. by 20-in. poster. Depending on your copy shop, this can take as little as 1 hour or up to 3 days, so plan accordingly.

5. Once you get the poster home, it's time to laminate it to the foam board. Please do this in a well-ventilated area or outside! Spray an even, thin layer of adhesive onto the surface of the foam board. Carefully align the top left-hand corner of your poster to the foam board and press the paper onto the board, keeping the edges aligned (drawing A). Smooth out any wrinkles as you move along. The adhesive dries pretty fast, so you'll need to work quickly.

6. Let the adhesive dry for about 1 hour before you handle the board again. This helps prevent the print from smudging if it gets too damp from the adhesive.

A.

7. Now, take the Crop-A-Dile and punch two holes in the sign, one on the top left corner and one on the top right corner, about 1 in. down and in from each edge.

8. The last step is to attach the finished sign to your getaway-mobile with ribbon (drawing B). How it's attached really depends on the car. Most often, it's easiest to tie a long piece of ribbon around the trunk's door and secure it to the sign. You may have to get creative with places to tie the ribbon, so be sure to practice on the car before the big day.

B.

tips & hints

- *Remember, Microsoft Word is different for PCs and Macs, so if you're having problems, click on Help for assistance.*

- *When designing your sign, go for high contrast between the background color and font color so the sign is readable as you go whizzing by. If you choose a thinner font or more subtle color combinations, make sure to size the wording large enough so that all and sundry can read that you are newlyweds!*

- *Sometimes copy shops can print signs onto foam board for you.*

This can be expensive so get a price quote before you commit to this option.

- *Depending on your car, ribbon may not be the most secure option for affixing the sign. Instead, use elastic thread (found at fabric shops) as a substitute for a snug fit on difficult surfaces.*

- *Before you commit to any specific printer, ask if there are any surcharges for full-bleed prints. Some printing services will charge more if you want a borderless print.*

Crafty Calculator

WHAT TO BUDGET

Printing	$20.00
Hole punch, eyelets	$10.00
Ribbon	$ 5.00
Total	$35.00

COST COMPARISON

Just-married banners cost upward of $50.00 for stock designs from wedding vendors. Ours, fully customized, is only $35.00.

STORE COST	YOUR COST
$50.00	**$35.00**

Post-Wedding Brunch Place Setting

Just imagine: You're married! Still on the high from the best day of your life, you're not too keen on letting the buzz fade away quite yet. You've got a free day or two before you head out on your honeymoon, so why not keep the festivities going by having a small, casual post-wedding brunch?

Short on time and cash to pull it off? No problem. Grab your leftover floral arrangements from your reception to adorn the tables. Serve light, make-ahead dishes (like yummy quiches or baked French toast), and add this place setting, complete with place mat, napkin ring, menu card, and menu pocket for super-easy decor. It's an instant party. Your guests will love to spend more quality time with you, and you and your husband get to hear over and over how wonderful your wedding was.

Time Wise

This truly is a simple set of projects that is suitable for crafters of any skill level. All of the elements of one place setting can be put together in less than 10 minutes.

A Little Me Time

This solo project is ideal for a low-key afternoon listening to tunes or after dinner while catching up on your favorite TV shows. Your wedding is only weeks away now, so you need all the relaxation you can get!

SUPPLIES

For the Place Mat
- Decorative paper, 12 in. by 12 in.
- Paper cutter

For the Napkin Ring
- Double-sided tape
- Patterned paper, 2 in. by 6 in.
- Napkin, cloth or paper

For the Menu Card
- Computer with Microsoft Word
- Printer
- Card stock, 4 in. by 6 in.

For the Menu Pocket
- Patterned card stock, 11 in. by 4$\frac{1}{2}$ in.
- Double-sided tape
- $\frac{1}{2}$-in.-wide ribbon, 6 in. to 8 in. long
- Bone folder

A.

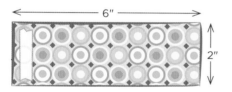

B.

DIRECTIONS

1. The first project is the easiest. For the place mat, all you'll need to do is trim a piece of decorative paper to 12 in. by 12 in. If you buy precut scrapbook paper (standard scrapbook paper is 12 in. by 12 in.) you may have to trim off a manufacturer's margin from the paper. Done! How easy was that?

2. Moving on to the napkin ring, you'll need to apply double-sided tape along the bottom of the short edge of the strip of patterned paper (drawing A). Gently bend the paper lengthwise into a circle and press the taped edge on top of the free end of the paper so that the edges overlap about $\frac{1}{4}$ in. (drawing B). Insert your napkin into the ring and, hey!, you're done with that part of the project, too.

3. Now it's time to tackle the menu cards. Open Microsoft Word and create a new document. Go to File and choose Page Setup. From the Paper Size bar, scroll down and select Manage Custom Sizes. On the bottom of the dialog box that appears, click the + button and enter "4 x 6" into this field. This creates a custom page size. In the fields on the right side of the dialog box, enter "6" for the height and "4" for the width. Use "0.25" for the top, bottom, left, and right margins. Click OK. This will drop you back to the Page Setup menu. Click the Portrait orientation, and then click OK again. You've just created the template for this 4-in. by 6-in. menu card.

4. Now it's time to insert the menu wording and any clip art into the menu card template. Once you've found the perfect combination of words, fonts, and layout, save your document and print your menu cards on the card stock.

5. The last task is to create the menu pocket. With a bone folder score the 11-in. by 4$\frac{1}{2}$-in. card stock widthwise, 4$\frac{3}{4}$ in. from the left end. Create another widthwise score line 1$\frac{1}{2}$ in. from the right end of the card stock (drawing C).

6. Fold the card stock along the 4$\frac{3}{4}$-in. score line. Fold the front flap at the 1$\frac{1}{2}$-in. score line down as well. Secure the sides of the pocket with double-sided tape (drawing D).

C.

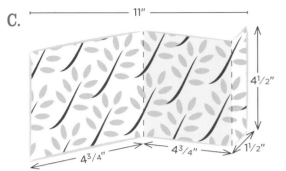

11"

4¹/₂"

4³/₄"

4³/₄"

1¹/₂"

D.

7. Attach a length of ribbon widthwise on the front of the pocket, over the front flap (see photo on p. 162 for positioning). Secure it with double-sided tape. Insert the menu into the pocket. Congrats! You just finished the entire project.

tips & hints

- Remember, Microsoft Word is different for PCs and Macs, so if you're having problems, click on Help for assistance.

- Scrapbook papers and card stock are excellent for this project. The standard 12-in. by 12-in. size makes it easy to measure and get multiple parts of the project out of a single sheet. They're also available in hundreds of patterns and colors to invoke any mood or theme you'd like.

- Higher-end scrapbook papers often have coordinating patterns on each side. This is great for adding a bit of whimsy to your place setting. Alternate the sides you use for different parts of the project. Contrast is fun!

- Remember to have extra blades for your paper cutter on hand. Paper will dull out your blades very quickly.

Crafty Calculator

WHAT TO BUDGET

Patterned papers	$50.00
Card stock	$ 5.00
Ribbon	$ 4.00
Tape	$ 4.00
Total (for 35 place settings)	**$63.00**

COST COMPARISON

It's almost impossible to find quality, matching place settings from party or stationery stores. From the limited number I found, coordinating place mats and napkin rings for 35 people cost about $200.00 total, or $5.00 per person. Our place setting, which includes a place mat, napkin holder, and menu pocket and card, will cost only $1.80 per person.

STORE COST	YOUR COST
$200.00	**$63.00**

6-2 Days to Go!

SWEET SEND-OFFS TO MARK THE OCCASION

Your final days of crafting are all about the little
details that will make your wedding truly special.
Yummy cookies and milk, charms and truffles, or
cupcake favors will indulge your guests without
breaking the bank. Custom-designed water-bottle
labels make a fashionable (and practical) statement
at each place setting. You'll want help from your
sanity-saving pals for the projects in this section, as
you'll be turning out favors in big numbers. Be sure
to reward them with delicious treats and cocktails (or
mocktails) while you get your craft on and enjoy your
last days of being in the unmarried demographic.

Cupcake in a Jar Favor

Vintage kitchen crafts rock my world. An avid home cook, I've been having fun resurrecting recipes that I made as a not-so-crafty kid and giving them a modern update.

Recently I rediscovered baking bread in a glass jar—something I did with my mom and grandma—and thought that it'd make an awesomely fun wedding favor. The DIY Bride twist replaces bread with the ever-popular cupcake. Who can resist cupcakes? Only those with no soul, I tell you.

This project takes serious prep time to do right—and to do safely. It is of the utmost importance to sterilize the jars to remove any contaminants left from manufacturing and shipping. Unsterilized jars will lead to moldy cupcakes or, even worse, food poisoning. Never, ever risk the health of your guests! That's just bad etiquette.

Time Wise

For this project you'll need 4 hours total. Expect to spend 1 hour or more sterilizing the jars and lids. Add in 1 hour to 2 hours of baking and cooling time for the cupcakes. Top it off with about 5 minutes of decorating per jar. Start at least 2 days ahead of the reception to allow enough time to prep, cook, and decorate.

Divide & Conquer

Grab a few kitchen-friendly pals to prep the jars and decorate the cupcakes.

SUPPLIES

- ½-pint, wide-mouth canning jars with lids
- Drying rack
- 1 box of cake mix or your favorite cupcake recipe (as long as it doesn't require baking at higher than 350°F)
- Towel or paper towels
- Nonstick baking spray, butter, or shortening
- All-purpose flour
- Ladle or measuring cup
- Baking sheet
- Silpat® fiberglass mat or parchment paper
- Cooling rack
- Buttercream frosting
- Small spatula or pastry bag and round tip, or quart-size resealable plastic bag
- Card stock or decorative paper, at least 8½ in. by 11 in.
- Circle cutter or scissors
- Double-sided tape
- ¼-in. grosgrain ribbon, about 12 in. long
- Miniature wooden spoon, found at craft stores

A.

DIRECTIONS

1. The first step is to sterilize the jars and lids to kill any bacteria or other contaminants. If you have a sanitation cycle in your dishwasher, run your lids and jars through a full cycle. Otherwise boil the jars and lids in a pot of water for 15 to 20 minutes. Make sure the jars are fully submersed so that all surfaces of the jar can be sterilized. After the jars have finished their boiling bath, set them aside on a rack to drain and completely cool.

2. Preheat the oven according to your cupcake recipe's directions. (Do not bake jars at a temperature higher than 350°F. Glass jars may shatter at high oven temps, and that's a very bad thing.)

3. Make your favorite cake batter according to the package or recipe directions. I used a yummy vanilla cake here but you can use any flavor you'd like.

4. Dry the sterilized jars with a clean, dry towel or a paper towel.

5. Next, coat the inside of the jar with nonstick cooking spray, and then flour the inside of the jars to prevent the cupcakes from sticking. Turn the jar on its side and rotate to disperse the flour over the spray. Shake the excess flour out of the jar.

6. Using a ladle or measuring cup, fill each jar about halfway with cupcake batter (drawing A). For the ½-pint jars I used, it takes just under ½ cup.

7. Place the filled jars on a baking sheet. I put a silicone Silpat mat underneath my jars to catch any spills and to help heat the jars evenly. You don't need a Silpat, but they also make cleaning up spills wonderfully easy. If you don't have one, no problem! Simply place a layer of parchment paper on the baking sheet underneath the jars.

8. Place the jars in the oven. Bake as directed. I recommend starting to check your cupcakes after 15 minutes and then every 5 minutes or so thereafter until they are done. Test to see if they are done by inserting a toothpick into the center of the cupcake (if it comes out clean, the cupcakes are done), or use the recommended test from your recipe.

9. Pull the baking sheet out of the oven and set it on a rack to cool. Beware: the glass jars are hot. Like sear-your-skin-right-off hot. Be very careful!

10. Once your jars o' cake are cool, you're free to frost them. I recommend a nice buttercream. I used a small spatula to frost the cupcakes (drawing B), but feel free to use a pastry bag with a round pastry tip or a resealable plastic bag. Don't forget to sample your tasty treats! Quality control is important, right?

B.

11. Dry your sterilized lids and lid rings with a clean towel. Now you're free to decorate the jars!

6
5
4
3
2
Days to go!

C.

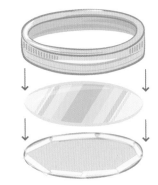

D.

12. I adorned the top of the cupcake jars with a custom top. First, trace a jar lid onto the decorative paper. Then use either a 2½-in. circle cutter or scissors (with a steady hand) to cut out the circle. Secure the paper to the lid with double-sided tape (drawing C). Of course, you can decorate your jar any way you'd like. Don't be afraid to experiment with label papers that have an adhesive back, wallpapers, fabrics, or whatever materials make your heart sing. Place the lid on the jar and screw on the lid ring.

13. To finish decorating your jar, add a length of ¼-in. grosgrain ribbon around the lid (drawing D). Measure the circumference of your lids to see how much ribbon you need. I used about 12 in. of ribbon total to overlap the ends and tie it all up on my jars. For a little something extra, thread a cute little wooden spoon onto the ribbon before tying a simple knot. Cut the edges of the ribbon at an angle for a nice, finished look.

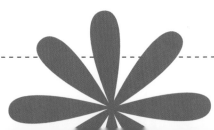

tips & hints

- Store your finished cupcakes in a cool, dry place. When the jar is sealed properly, cupcakes will stay moist and yummy for several days. Some people will say even weeks, but I wouldn't push it for more than 5 days max. If you use a buttercream recipe that contains milk, I'd only go a couple of days. It's best to keep the cupcakes in a refrigerator or cooler to help keep them fresh and unspoiled (and check them before handing them out, just to be safe).

- Use wide-mouthed jars for best results. Don't put more than 1 cup of batter in any jar because the batter might not cook evenly or cook all the way through. Uncooked batter equals potential food poisoning. Not a fun favor for your guests!

- Before you bake an entire batch of cupcakes, do a test run with a single jar to get a feel for how much batter and baking time you need. Ovens and cake recipes or mixes can vary greatly.

- I accidentally overfilled my jars when I tested out this project. The cakes were puffing up over the tops of the jars. To fix them, I used a serrated knife to trim off the excess cake while the cakes were still hot (using an oven mitt to hold the jars). As the cakes cooled they shrunk to just the right size. You'll want about $1/8$ in. to $1/4$ in. of space between the top of the cake and the top of the jar to allow for precious frosting.

Days to go!

6
5
4
3
2

Crafty Calculator

WHAT TO BUDGET

Jar and lid	$0.85
Decorative paper	$0.20
Ribbon	$0.10
Wooden spoon	$0.05
Cake ingredients	$0.35
Total per cupcake	$ 1.55

COST COMPARISON

High-end bakeries charge around $4.00 for a simple cupcake without packaging. Your utterly delicious DIY cupcake—complete with decorated jar—will cost you about $1.55 each.

STORE COST	YOUR COST
$4.00	**$1.55**

Milk & Cookies Favor

Okay, seriously, who doesn't love milk and cookies? Imagine the surprise and delight your guests will express when they realize they get these yummy goodies as a thank-you gift at your wedding. Compared to the tired and boring edibles most of us have experienced as wedding favors, this is a welcome—and unexpected—treat. Your guests are worth more than imprinted chocolate candies or Jordan almonds. This is a playful way to show your appreciation.

The beauty of this project is that it can be as DIY as you'd like it to be. Store-bought cookies can easily be replaced with your super-secret to-die-for cookies that are fresh from your very own oven. A single sheet of 12-in.-square paper can be used for decorating both elements of the favor, or you can mix and match papers to fit your one-of-a-kind design scheme.

Time Wise

Once your template is ready to go, each milk carton and cookie bag combo takes about 10 minutes to create.

Divide & Conquer

Many hands will make light work of this project. Grab a few helpers (just tell them about the cookies), put on your favorite high-energy playlist, and enjoy an afternoon of delicious favor fun.

SUPPLIES

- ¹/₂-pint carton of milk
- Pencil
- Paper for template
- Paper cutter
- Scissors
- Patterned paper, 12 in. by 12 in.
- Matching or coordinating patterned paper, 12 in. by 12 in.
- Double-sided tape
- Heavy-duty hole punch or Crop-A-Dile tool
- ¹/₄-in.-wide ribbon, about 6 in. long
- Cookies of your choice, 2 to 3 per favor
- Small plastic treat bags for the cookies, 4 in. by 6 in.
- Stapler

DIRECTIONS

1. The first step is making a stylish paper wrap to cover the milk carton. Because the dimensions of ¹/₂-pint milk containers can vary a bit from dairy to dairy, you'll need to measure one of your cartons to get the exact size of your carton (drawing A). Measure the length and height of all four sides and top of the carton. Increase each measurement just slightly so that the patterned paper wrap will cover the carton when it is folded.

2. Once your measurements are recorded, create a template of your carton's dimensions on a regular piece of printer paper. Cut this out and trace it onto the back of the patterned paper (drawing B). Use a paper cutter or scissors to cut out the milk carton wrap. Before you cut out the rest of the paper for the cartons, loosely wrap the paper around the carton to make sure your measurements are correct. Make adjustments if necessary and cut out the rest of the wraps.

3. Place a strip of double-sided tape along the edge of one side of the milk carton. Stick the corresponding end of the patterned paper wrap to the tape and wrap the rest of the paper around the carton. Secure the free end of paper to the carton with another piece of double-sided tape. Press along the corners so that the paper conforms to the shape of the box.

4. Now that the paper is secured along the sides of the carton, fold the paper along the contours of the upper parts of the carton and secure it at the top with double-sided tape. Punch two holes in the top of the carton about 1 in. apart and about ¹/₄ in. from the top of the carton (drawing C), being careful not to puncture the carton's seal. Spoiled or leaking milk is no fun!

A.

B.

C.

D.

5. Now thread the ribbon through the holes you punched by inserting one end of ribbon into each of the holes and pulling them tight and even (drawing D). Cross the ribbon from the left-hand hole over to the right and put it back through the right-hand hole, and pull it out from the other side. Then do the same for the ribbon on the right side.

6. From paper that matches or coordinates with the paper you wrapped the milk cartons in, cut a strip long enough and wide enough to span the top of your plastic treat bags. I used a 2-in. by 4-in. piece for my 4-in. by 6-in. bags. Fold the strip in half lengthwise and set aside.

7. Place the cookies into the treat bags. Fold down the tops of the bags once or twice. Staple them shut. Add the folded paper strips you just cut to the tops of the bags, securing them in place with double-sided tape. That's it!

tips & hints

- *For obvious safety reasons, always keep your milk refrigerated! When decorating the cartons, work in small bunches, pulling out only enough cartons from the fridge that you can complete within 10 minutes max.*

- *At the reception, keep the milk cartons in the fridge until it's time to serve them or time for your guests to go home. Don't put them directly on ice. The melting ice will get your paper wet.*

- *Mix and match patterns and colors of paper and ribbon for your own unique look.*

Crafty Calculator

WHAT TO BUDGET

Milk, 12 case	$0.50
Paper	$0.58
Ribbon	$0.25
Cookies	$0.50
Plastic bags	$0.25
Total for 12 favors	$2.08

COST COMPARISON

Caterers charge around $50.00 for a dozen cookie favors, and that's without any decorated cartons of milk. Your custom-designed creations complete with cookies and milk will cost half that amount.

STORE COST	YOUR COST
$4.16	$2.08

Customized Water Bottle Label

Bottled water is a must at every wedding bar, but couldn't it at least be nice to look at while it's on display? The answer: Of course it can! We're crafters. We can make nearly anything look good.

In our quest to brand our big day, the often-ugly water bottle has become the latest recipient of a wedding makeover. With just a few supplies, turning a plastic bottle into a fashion statement is a cinch. Who knew quenching thirst could be so stylish? And let's not forget to be green! Consider creating a larger customized label for a recycling bin.

Time Wise

Once the manufacturer's labels are removed and your design is finished, you should be able to complete at least half a dozen bottles in under 30 minutes.

It's a Girl Thing

While you can create and print the labels on your own, gather your bridesmaids together for assembly. Satisfy their thirst with a bubbly drink and a few yummy snacks, and they'll be happy to help and leave asking when the next crafting session is!

SUPPLIES

- Water bottles
- Ruler
- Computer with Microsoft Word
- Printer
- Clip art, print quality of 300 dpi or more
- Glossy printer paper suitable for your printer
- Paper cutter or scissors
- Double-sided tape

A.

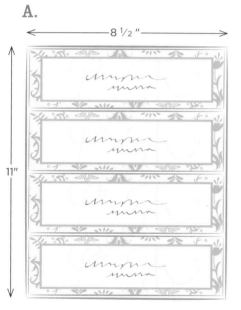

DIRECTIONS

1. The first step to creating water bottle couture is to peel off the manufacturer's labels from the bottles (or cut them off with scissors if they're proving to be stubborn). Save one of the labels to measure for your template.

2. Because water bottle labels vary in size and shape from manufacturer to manufacturer, you'll need to create your very own template to fit your brand of bottle. Measure the label you saved in Step 1.

3. Open Microsoft Word and create a new document. Create a text box in the dimensions of the water bottle label you just measured. To adjust the size of the box, double click on it and a dialog box will pop up in which you can input the exact dimensions you need in the Size tab.

4. Insert a piece of clip art into the text box by dragging and dropping the image with your mouse. This will be your background image. Don't be afraid to experiment with clip art. Get creative by layering and combining colors and designs to make something totally unique. Check out the Resources (p. 214) for the best spots to score stylish, print-ready clip art.

5. Create another text box for any text you'd like to include on your label. Drag it on top of the first text box. Double-click on it to bring up the Formatting dialog box and adjust the size, color, border size, and style of the box. You can create multiple layers and multiple boxes to add text or graphics to your unique design. Just keep everything within the size of the original label–size text box, so nothing gets cut off come printing time.

6. Copy and paste all the boxes until you have a full page of labels, leaving a small margin between each one (drawing A). The idea is to fit as many copies as you can on one sheet without overlapping the design. Save the document and print the labels onto glossy paper and set them aside to dry.

7. Using a paper cutter, cut the labels from the glossy paper.

8. Place strips of double-sided tape on the back of the label (drawing B) and wrap the label around the bottle, pressing the tape firmly in place (drawing C).

B.

C.

6
5
4
3
2

Days to go!

tips & hints

- *Remember, Microsoft Word is different for PCs and Macs, so if you're having problems, click on Help for assistance.*

- *Ink-jet printer ink usually takes a few minutes to set on glossy papers so beware of smudges! Allow the ink to fully dry before cutting or affixing the labels.*

- *Sticker paper also works well for this project, but I found it harder to control when wrapping it around the bottles.*

- *The labels are not water resistant. They will smudge, tear, and fall apart if you put them in a cooler full of ice. They will be okay if they're refrigerated.*

- *Clip art must be print quality (300 dpi) to look good. Most free clip art on the Internet is made for web use and is only 72 dpi, which won't print well. Suitable clip art can be found at online stock illustration sites such as Istockphoto℠ for a small fee. Thousands of designs are available and can be used in your other wedding projects like invitations, aisle runners, and thank-you cards.*

- *Keep an eye out at your local grocery store for sales on bottled water to help cut costs.*

Crafty Calculator

WHAT TO BUDGET

Water bottles	$35.00
Glossy paper	$20.00
Clip art	$10.00
Total (for 100 bottles)	$65.00

COST COMPARISON

Custom water bottle labels alone— no water bottle—start around $1.00 per label. You can create ultra-stylish designs at home for just $0.65— including the water bottle!

STORE COST	YOUR COST
$1.00	**65¢**

Vineyard Charm & Truffle Favor

Living near the Napa Valley wine country, I'm lucky enough to participate in a number of vineyard-themed events every year. They tend to be rustic and elegant at the same time, combining the casual California vineyard vibe with the sophistication of metropolitan wine events.

Finding favors that reflect such a unique combination of styles can be a challenge. My solution is an easy one: Spoil your guests with shiny wine-related trinkets and ultra-yummy chocolates. Treating them to these little indulgences is a divine way to show your appreciation, and, really, is there any combination more decadent than wine and chocolate? (The answer is no.)

Time Wise

Assembling each wine charm takes 10 minutes to 15 minutes, depending on skill level. Tack on 15 minutes to 30 minutes to put the whole ensemble together.

Divide & Conquer

I'm never surprised by how quickly girls on a mission can get things done. Whip up a batch of brownies and invite your best buds over to help you eat them and to tackle the truffle favors (the brownies will ease the temptation to eat all the truffles!). You'll have fabulous favors in no time.

SUPPLIES

Truffle Box
- For the box, 1 in. wide by 2 in. long and 1 in. high
- Tissue paper
- Homemade or gourmet truffles
- ¼-in.-wide ribbon, about 8 in. long
- Scissors

Vineyard Charm
- For the gold seed beads, size 11/0
- 1-in. gold wire earring hoops
- Needle-nose pliers
- 24-gauge gold jewelry wire
- Wire cutters
- Purple seed beads, size 8/0

STATION 1: BOX ASSEMBLY
Although it's possible to box-make from scratch, I wouldn't advise it, especially if you have lots of favors to make. Check out a local craft retailer or online paper specialty store for cute, small, inexpensive boxes that echo or complement your wedding colors or theme. Have a few girls fold up the boxes and line them with tissue paper.

STATION 2: CHARM MAKERS
Put the nimblest crafters on this station making the vineyard charms.

STATION 3: FINAL ASSEMBLY
One or two girls should be able to handle packaging the truffles, tying the boxes with ribbon, and attaching the charms.

DIRECTIONS

1. Assemble or fold the truffle boxes according to the manufacturer's instructions. Line them with tissue paper, and set aside.

2. For the vineyard charm, slide gold seed beads onto the wire earring hoop. Fill almost the entire hoop, leaving just a little space for the beads to slide around a bit. You'll need this bit of space to attach the beaded grape cluster later on. Once your earring hoop is nearly full of beads, use a pair of needle-nose pliers to bend the regular end of the hoop (the one without the hole) up to a 45° angle. This will prevent the beads from sliding off the hoop and keep the charm closed around a wineglass stem when it's in use. Set the beaded rings aside and get started on those adorable grape clusters!

3. Cut a 4-in. length of gold wire. Fold it in half to make a crease in the middle (drawing A) and string 21 purple beads onto the wire (drawing B).

4. Count inward to the center-most bead (the 11th) and, holding it between your thumb and index finger, twist it twice so that the wire is tightly wrapped just above the bead (drawing C).

5. This is where the project gets tricky. You'll now twist the two sides of the wired hoop around each other a few times in a spiral motion. Hold the top of the wire hoop with one hand, and with the index finger and thumb of the other hand grab the bottom of the hoop. Twist the bottom of the hoop around and around—this will bring the wires together as a single unit and bunch up the beads to create the cluster (drawing D). The tighter you twist, the better the bunch will look.

6. Wrap one end of the wire tightly around the base of the beaded gold hoop a few times, between some of the beads (drawing E). Cut off any excess.

7. The last step of your lovely vineyard charm is to wrap the remaining end of the wire around one of the round barrels of your pliers. This will create a cute tendril (drawing E)—just like a real grapevine!

A.

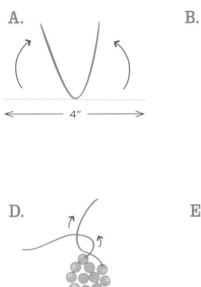

← 4" →

B.

C.

D.

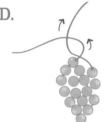

E.

8. Now add one or two truffles (depending on the box size) to each tissue paper-lined box. Wrap the truffle box with a beautiful ribbon and attach your handmade vineyard charm into the knot, just before you make a bow.

tips & hints

- *I felt that one charm per guest was sufficient, but do feel free to do them in pairs if your time, budget, and guest list is manageable.*

- *Making the grape clusters can take a few tries to get just right. Don't get discouraged! Take a deep breath and just experiment and play with the materials until it looks and feels right.*

Crafty Calculator

WHAT TO BUDGET

Gold hoops	$0.25
Gold beads	$0.10
Purple beads	$0.12
Box	$0.40
Ribbon	$0.30
Tissue paper	$0.05
Truffles	$1.00
Total (per favor)	$2.22

COST COMPARISON

Prices for gourmet truffles and custom-made chocolates can vary widely in the retail market. For quality chocolates and wine charms, expect to pay about $3.00 per favor, and add at least $1.00 for a handcrafted wine charm. Our version costs just $2.22 to create at home.

STORE COST	YOUR COST
$4.00	**$2.22**

1

Day to go!

1 Day to Go!

FORGET-ME-NOT DETAILS

It's down to 24 hours! Can you believe how far you've come? The last projects you'll be putting your hands on are the ones that need to be done as close to the wedding day as possible. The projects in this section have flowers and food, both perishable, and will need your (or your designated helpers') attention today. The Carnation Pomander is both gorgeous and versatile. Use it as a centerpiece, aisle marker, or bouquet substitute. And a popcorn buffet is the perfect alternative to a dessert table. Let your guests choose from salty, savory, and sweet—yum! Be sure to start your projects early enough in the day in case you need to run out for extra supplies or get sidetracked deliriously celebrating your soon-to-be status.

Carnation Pomander

Carnations, my friends, are the most maligned wedding flowers, and their bad rep is wholly undeserved. Sure, they've been included in tacky arrangements and cheap-o supermarket bins (usually dyed hideous shades of blue or green for an extra "festive" vibe), but carnations are a truly stunning flower—not unlike the peonies, roses, and other posh flowers that can cost a small fortune.

For you carnation naysayers, this project will change your mind and elevate the humble carnation into elite flower status. Behold the pomander, possibly the hottest all-around accessory for weddings. Some of my favorite pomander uses are as alternatives to bouquets and

Time Wise

Once your foam has soaked for 2 hours and your flowers are prepped, it should take about 1 hour to create each pomander.

Divide & Conquer

This project is perfect for your crafty maids with green thumbs. Ask them to tackle it the night before or morning of your big day (though preferably not in their bridesmaids' dresses!).

SUPPLIES

- Floral foam block, 3 in. by 4 in. by 9 in., or topiary ball, 10 in. to 18 in. in circumference
- Large bucket of water or sink to soak floral balls and hydrate flowers
- Carnations, 24 to 30 medium blooms for 10-in. foam balls; 36 large for 18-in. balls
- Floral shears
- Ribbon
- Floral pins

A.

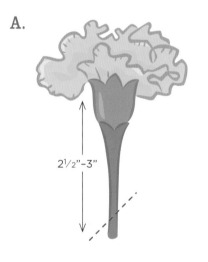

2½"–3"

B.

flower-girl baskets (simply hold the pomander by the attached ribbon). I also adore them hung with a ribbon from the reception ceiling, in all different colors and sizes. Then there's displaying them on top of glass vases as centerpieces. Oh! How about mini pomanders hung from chairs or used with shepherd's hooks as aisle markers? Carnation pomanders make a bold statement, are easy to assemble, and can be used in tons of ways. What's not to love?

DIRECTIONS

1. Soak the floral foam ball in water for a few hours. Usually 2 hours is sufficient.

2. While the floral balls are soaking, start prepping your flowers. This can take longer than you might think! First, grab a handful of flowers and cut their stems at a 45° angle about 2½ in. to 3 in. from the bottom of the bloom (drawing A). Remove any leaves or thorns that remain on the stems. Put the flowers in water while you trim the stems of the next bunch of flowers, so that all the buds stay hydrated and fresh while you work.

3. Once the foam ball is hydrated, create a hanger for the pomander. The easiest way to do this is to cut a length of ribbon, about 10 in. for a 10-in. ball. Fold it in half to make a 5-in. loop. Secure the ends of the loop with floral pins onto the top of the pomander (drawing B).

4. Once all of your flowers are cut, the hanger is in place, and your foam ball has been hydrated, it's time to start assembling the pomander. Starting at the top

of the ball beside the ribbon hanger, insert flower stems directly into the foam, all the way down to the bloom (drawing C). I like to move in a left to right pattern, from top to bottom. This step is wet and messy—be prepared!

5.   Stop occasionally to check to see that the flowers are more or less evenly placed around the ball and that they all sit at the same height. If one section starts to look crowded or sparse, it's best to make adjustments early on in the process. Continue until the pomander is fully covered with blooms. You're done—how fab is that?

C.

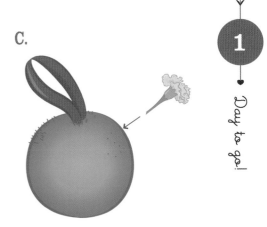

1

Day to go!

tips & hints

- *Depending on the time of your ceremony and reception, this is a night-before or day-of project, and one that you'll need to handoff to a trusted helper. A conservative estimate is a 1-hour assembly time for each medium-size pomander. Plan accordingly!*

- *Make sure your flowers are fully bloomed for the best results. Depending on the type, you may need to buy the flowers 2 days or more in advance. Check with your floral supplier to determine the best delivery time for you.*

- *Carnations aren't the only flowers you can use! Hydrangeas, roses, stephanotis, mums, peonies, and lilies are all excellent choices for pomanders.*

- *Broken flower stem? No problem! Insert a toothpick or bamboo skewer into the head of the flower to create a makeshift stem.*

Crafty Calculator

WHAT TO BUDGET

Carnations (36 stems)	$22.00
Floral foam ball	$ 4.00
Ribbon	$ 3.00
Total	$29.00

COST COMPARISON

Florists will charge anywhere from $45.00 to more than $100.00 for carnation pomanders. With just a little help, you can make a 10-in. pomander for much less.

STORE COST	YOUR COST
$100.00	**$29.00**

Asian Rock & Bamboo Centerpiece

If peace and tranquility are what you seek for your wedding's vibe, then there's no more perfect theme than Asian design. With clean, simple lines and minimal, modern shapes, a Japanese-inspired reception is sure to put you and your guests into a Zen-like state of bliss.

This centerpiece is a personal favorite of mine. I use it for special occasions at home because it not only is easy and economical to put together, it's also absolutely stunning in its simplicity.

Assembly of the centerpieces couldn't be easier, but when doing them in bulk you will want a few helping hands to finish up the project in a timely fashion.

Time Wise

This is a super-easy project. Once your bamboo is prepped, expect to complete anywhere from 5 to 10 centerpieces in 30 minutes.

It's a Girl Thing

This is a great project to hand off to one or two of your maids the day before your wedding. They can handle the final assembly at the reception while you primp and preen before the ceremony.

SUPPLIES

- Lucky bamboo, 4 stalks, available at garden centers and online
- Floral knife
- Container of water
- Shallow vase, round or square, about 2 in. high and 8 in. to 10 in. in diameter
- Black river rocks, available at garden centers and craft stores
- Pitcher or container of water with a pour spout
- Gardenia with stem cut

DIRECTIONS

1. The preparation for the centerpieces is very easy. Begin by trimming the bottom ends of the lucky bamboo stalks with a floral knife. You'll want the ends as level as possible to help them stand upright in the vases. After you've cut each stalk, put them in a container filled with about 1 in. of water until you're ready to use them. This can be done 2 to 3 days in advance.

2. When it's time to assemble the centerpieces, it's best to do each one at the table where it'll be displayed to prevent the bamboo from tipping over. Cover the bottom of the vase with a single layer of rocks. Insert individual stalks of lucky bamboo into the vase. Add more rocks around the bases of the stalks to keep them upright and secure.

3. Gently add 1 in. or so of water to the vase. Using a pitcher or container with a spout helps you avoid splashing water on your pristinely set reception tables and gives you better control over how much water comes out.

4. The final step is to put a gardenia in the water.

tips & hints

- Lucky bamboo (not really bamboo but a member of the lily family) is really hardy. You can easily purchase your stalks 1 week ahead of time and keep them in a warm 65°F to 70°F room until needed; just add a little water to the bottom of the container.

- Home and garden centers sometimes carry lucky bamboo, but the best buys for bulk orders are found online. Check out the Resources (p. 214) for recommended vendors.

- Gardenias are beautiful flowers, but have a strong scent and are somewhat pricey. Don't hesitate to use silk flowers if the smell or cost bothers you. If you want to sub in another fresh flower, look for ones with waxy petals. Orchids, stephanotis, water lilies, and roses are good choices.

- Floating candles are a brilliant substitution when flowers won't work for you, but if you decide to go with an open-flame alternative, follow the instructions for the candles' use and make sure they aren't left unattended.

Crafty Calculator

WHAT TO BUDGET

Glass vase	$10.00
Flowers	$ 9.00
Rocks (2-lb. bag)	$ 3.00
Lucky bamboo (4 stalks)	$ 4.00
Total for centerpiece	**$26.00**

COST COMPARISON

Expect to pay anywhere from $45.00 to more than $60.00 for a simple Japanese-inspired centerpiece from a florist. Your one-of-a-kind creation will cost only $26.00.

STORE COST	YOUR COST
$60.00	**$26.00**

Gourmet Popcorn Buffet

Here's an experiment for you: Stick a bag of popcorn in the microwave at work. After it has finished popping, look at the clock and time how long it takes for your co-workers to come out of their cubicle-induced stupor to proclaim you as their new best friend.

Popcorn is the siren song of snack foods, a lure to the most jaded of munchers. If you're looking for a yummy alternative to the overdone and often expensive candy buffet for your reception, popcorn is your budget-friendly, ultra-delicious solution that's sure to please your picky pals.

This project is great for beginners and when you might be short on time. The trickiest part is keeping the popcorn fresh until reception day. Resealable plastic bags are a perfect storage solution and allow you to make your popcorn creations up to 3 days ahead of time.

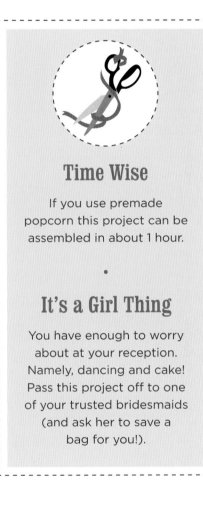

Time Wise

If you use premade popcorn this project can be assembled in about 1 hour.

It's a Girl Thing

You have enough to worry about at your reception. Namely, dancing and cake! Pass this project off to one of your trusted bridesmaids (and ask her to save a bag for you!).

SUPPLIES

- Galvanized tin containers, one for each kind of popcorn
- Popped popcorn, in different flavors, approximately 5 cups per tin
- Patterned paper strips, 1½ in. high
- Paper cutter
- Double-sided tape
- Small paper bags with an inner plastic lining, found at party supply and craft stores in the food or candy-making aisles
- Computer with Microsoft Word
- Printer
- White card stock, 8½ in. by 11 in.

A.

B.

DIRECTIONS

1. Because the popcorn will be coming into direct contact with the container, the first step is to thoroughly clean the tin containers with a solution of 1 part bleach to 10 parts water. This will destroy any bacteria that may be lurking inside. Rinse with water and allow the containers to dry completely.

2. Now it's time to decorate the popcorn bags. Cut strips of patterned paper 1½-in. high, making sure the width spans that of the bag. For simplicity, I decorate just the front of the bags, but you can decorate all four sides of the bags or front and back if you'd like (photo A).

3. Apply double-sided tape to the back of the patterned paper strips and apply them to the front of the bags, midway from the top and bottom.

4. Now it's time to make the labels for the popcorn tins so your guests aren't guessing what the mystery popcorn flavors are. Open Microsoft Word and create a new document. Create a 4-in.-wide by 3-in.-high text box for each popcorn flavor you'll be using. This is an approximate size to fit the tins in my example. Don't be afraid to scale your labels to better fit your containers! Click inside the text box with your mouse and insert the popcorn flavor name. Print the labels onto white card stock and cut out them out.

5. Cut pieces of patterned paper ½ in. larger in length and width than the popcorn labels you just created in step 4. Place strips of double-sided tape on the back of the flavor labels and attach them to the pieces of patterned paper, centering them in the middle of the paper to create a nice, even border on all sides (photo B). Use double-sided tape to attach the finished labels to the popcorn containers.

6. The popcorn is next. Whether you use homemade, microwave, or store-bought popcorn, keep your popped corn in a tightly sealed plastic bag until it's ready to use.

7. Now, for the ridiculously easy setup! At the reception, set containers on a table. Fill them with the popcorn. Open the paper bags and set them near the popcorn containers. Be sure to provide scoops or spoons for each container so that your guests aren't tempted to put their hands in the popcorn. That's not good eats!

tips & hints

- *For this project, I used galvanized buckets because they have a rustic, casual feel to them. You can use any container for yours (just remember to clean it thoroughly before filling it with the popcorn). Check out apothecary jars, tin pails, terra-cotta pots, milk glasses, ceramics, and wood baskets (with a lining to prevent splinters) as alternatives to fit your personal style.*

- *I used salted, butter and caramel, and cheddar popcorn, but don't be afraid to serve your own mix of yummy flavors.*

- *It's best not to use real butter or margarine on the popcorn. Anything wet will make the popcorn soggy. Try dry butter-flavored seasonings instead.*

- *For extra flavor, set out shakers of seasonings for guests to create their own signature flavors. Try fun combinations like cinnamon-sugar, chipotle-cilantro, and parmesan-garlic. (Make labels for the spice shakers just like you did for the popcorn containers for a super-cute put-together look!)*

Crafty Calculator

WHAT TO BUDGET

Tin containers	$32.00
Popcorn	$15.00
Bags	$14.00
Paper	$12.00
Total (serves 100)	**$73.00**

COST COMPARISON

For just $73.00, you can provide 100 guests with a tasty popcorn favor. While most caterers don't provide popcorn buffets, the ones who do typically charge about $200.00 to feed the same size crowd.

STORE COST	YOUR COST
$200.00	$73.00

6

Hours to go!

6 Hours to Go!

FINISHING TOUCHES FOR THE SPECIAL DAY

Congratulations, intrepid do-it-yourselfer. You've made it through an entire year of planning and crafting the most personal wedding on the face of the planet—yours! Today's the day to let a handful of trusted helpers work on the finishing touches that will make your day fabulous. This section has the details that your friends and family will need to put together a beautiful bouquet, a lovely lime centerpiece, and a totally fun photo booth. Now take a deep breath, hand off this book, and enjoy the fruits of your labor. You deserve it, you beautiful bride!

Lily Bloom Bouquet

There are times when a bride just has to splurge. Maybe it's for the ornately embellished and boxed invitations. Oftentimes it's for an over-the-top handcrafted tiara. And sometimes there's a do-it-yourself project so beautifully brilliant that one just can't resist it. This is one of those projects.

For any bride (or maid) who wants to carry a unique and bold bouquet, this is a winner. This oh-so-clever project creates a single, large flower bloom out of individual petals from an Oriental lily.

Beauty comes with a price, however. This project must be made on the day of the wedding. Brides, please do *not* attempt to do this yourselves. Enlist the help of a trusted crafty pal to do this as a wedding present to you, and you'll be so glad you did when you have this stunning bouquet in hand as you walk down the aisle.

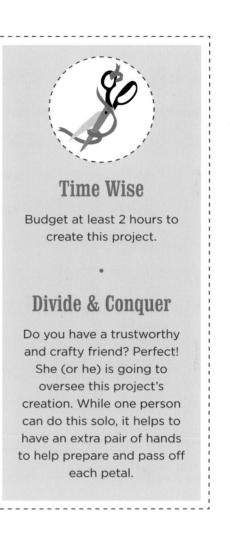

Time Wise

Budget at least 2 hours to create this project.

•

Divide & Conquer

Do you have a trustworthy and crafty friend? Perfect! She (or he) is going to oversee this project's creation. While one person can do this solo, it helps to have an extra pair of hands to help prepare and pass off each petal.

SUPPLIES

- 40 Oriental lilies, in full bloom
- Buckets of water to hold the lilies
- Paper towels
- Floral shears
- Floral wire
- Wire cutters
- Floral tape
- 1-in.-wide ribbon, 4 yd.
- Floral pins

DIRECTIONS

1. Get started by plucking the stamen from the center of each lily. This holds potent pollen that will stain everything it touches. Gently pull it out with a paper towel and discard it in the trash.

2. Next, carefully remove the petals from each lily's stem. Leave one flower intact, though. You'll need this as the center, or starting point, for the bouquet later on. Set the petals on a layer of cool, damp paper towels to help keep them hydrated and to prevent bruising.

3. After you've removed the petals of about 30 lilies, it's time to start gathering and wrapping them with floral tape and wire. Cut an 18-in. length of floral wire. Place one end of the wire on the inner base of a lily petal (drawing A). Wrap floral tape around the area where the wire and petal meet to secure it in place (drawing B). Wire and wrap all of the petals this way.

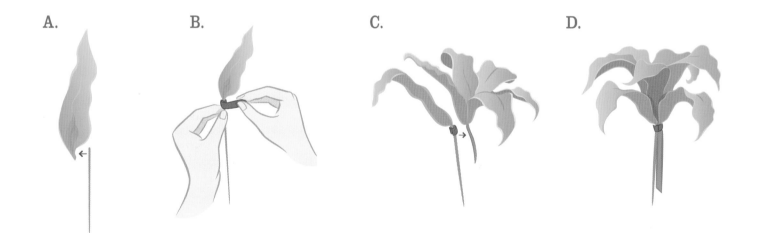

A.   B.   C.   D.

4. Once the petals are wired, it's time to put the bouquet together. Start with the intact lily you set aside earlier. In a circular direction, start adding individual wired petals around the bloom in a single ring (drawing C). After each ring of petals is in place, secure it with floral tape (drawing D), and then circle around the bouquet with another layer of petals. Each time around, the bouquet will hold a few more petals than the previous one as it expands in size.

5. After all of your petals are in place, wrap the loose wires together with floral tape to create a single, solid stem. You may need to trim the stem down to the size that best fit your hands. That's fine. Use your wire cutters to snip the wires.

6. To cover the floral-taped wire handle, wrap a pretty ribbon around it and secure it with a pretty bow. Use floral pins to keep the ribbon in place.

tips & hints

- *For a medium bouquet, expect to use around 30 Oriental lilies or 40 Asiatic lilies. Remember that lily petals can be fragile. Have plenty of extra flowers on hand in case any of your petals tear or bruise. I recommend ordering 10 percent more than you think you'll need.*

- *Keep the lilies in water until you're ready to use them.*

- *Lilies are quite fragrant. If you (or anyone in your bridal party) are sensitive to scent, there are plenty of beautiful alternative flowers like Cymbidium orchids, amaryllis, and tulips. Fresh flowers not in your budget? Silks will work well for this bouquet.*

Crafty Calculator

WHAT TO BUDGET

40 Oriental lilies	$ 100.00
Floral wire	$ 4.50
Floral tape	$ 3.00
Ribbon	$ 5.00
Total	$ 112.50

COST COMPARISON

While this project does cost $112.50, that's still much, *much* less than what you'd pay a florist to create the same bouquet. Price quotes range from $180.00 to over $250.00 for a similar arrangement at floral design shops.

STORE COST	YOUR COST
$250.00	**$112.50**

Flower & Citrus Centerpiece

There are few do-it-yourself projects that strike fear into the hearts of soon-to-be newlyweds as much as centerpieces. You should see my e-mails, people! Every single day my inbox is inundated with frantic pleas for help, bribes for insider how-to info, recounts of recent centerpiece nightmares, and a plethora of "How do I make a Preston Bailey–type centerpiece on a tiny budget?"

Attaining the grandeur of his high holiness of event and floral design is no small feat for us mere mortals, but I can guide you in creating a vibrant, affordable centerpiece that'll dazzle all of the senses and make you look like a pro, too.

This citrus and floral centerpiece is one of my all-time favorite projects. Not only can it be done on a tight budget, but it's also easy to customize to fit nearly any theme.

Time Wise

Depending on your skill level, set aside 20 minutes to 40 minutes for each centerpiece. This includes lime and flower prep.

It's a Girl Thing

This is a great project to hand off to trusted crafty friends on your wedding day. They can handle the preparation while you're basking in your pre-ceremony pampering. One can handle slicing the limes and the other can prep the flowers. Both can work together assembling the final centerpieces.

SUPPLIES

- Clear square or rectangular vase, 5 in. to 8 in. tall
- Floral foam, 1 to 2 blocks, soaked in water for at least a few hours
- Ruler
- Flowers of your choice, 1 to 2 dozen
- Buckets of water for keeping flowers fresh
- Floral knife
- Limes, about 10
- Serrated kitchen knife
- Cutting board
- Pitcher of water

DIRECTIONS

1. Measure the inside of the vase and cut the floral foam block so that it is 1 in. smaller than the length and width of the vase and about half of the height. For example, if you have an 8-in.-tall vase that is 4 in. wide, the floral foam would be 4 in. tall and 3 in. wide. You may need multiple pieces of foam to accommodate the size and shape of the vase. Soak the foam in water for a few hours, or overnight.

2. Once the foam is hydrated, let it drain for a few minutes in a sink to remove excess water. You want the foam moist but not so wet that it will create puddles of water on your work surface.

3. While the foam is draining, prepare your flowers. Cut the stems at a 45° angle about 1 in. shorter than the height of the vase.

4. Place the foam in the bottom of your container. Center it. Insert the flowers directly into the foam. Fill the vase with about two-thirds of the flowers.

5. Grab the limes and cut them into $1/4$-in. slices, discarding the ends (drawing A). Begin adding lime slices between the floral foam and the sides of the vase. Layer the limes for a mosaic effect, making sure the flat (cut) sides of the lime slices face the glass (drawing B). Finish adding the flowers.

6. Once all the flowers are in place, fill the container with $3/4$ in. of water. Add any remaining lime slices to fill the vase. The water, flowers, and foam should keep the lime slices in place.

A.

B.

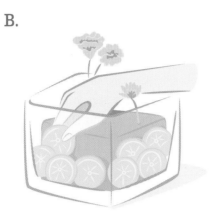

tips & hints

- *This is a day-of wedding project and not something that the bridal party should handle. Hand this off to a trusted helper, several hours before the ceremony.*

- *Limes can be cut a day ahead of time and should be kept in the refrigerator until use.*

- *I love to buy limes from local farmers' markets. I find I get a better deal—and larger limes.*

- *Other fruits or even vegetables can be used for this project. Oranges, grapefruit, uncut grapes or berries, celery, bell peppers, asparagus, and artichokes are all creative and unique options.*

- *Before you commit to a flower and citrus combination, do a test arrangement. Some flowers may discolor or wilt prematurely due to the acidity of the citrus.*

Crafty Calculator

WHAT TO BUDGET

Glass vase	$ 8.00
Floral foam	$ 1.50
Flowers	$20.00
Limes	$ 3.00
Total	$32.50

COST COMPARISON

Each centerpiece, using in-season flowers and fruits, will cost some $32.50 to make at home. Professional florists will charge anywhere from $45.00 to $80.00 for a fruit and flower centerpiece.

STORE COST	YOUR COST
$80.00	**$32.50**

DIY Photo Booth

If your friends and family are complete hams for the camera like mine are, then a photo booth is a must-have for your reception. Not only will you be able to capture priceless moments of your special day to remember for years to come, but you'll likely gather pretty darned good fuel for blackmail.

But seriously, photo booths are truly a great way to bring together your guests for one-of-a-kind shots that bring out the playful side of even your most camera-shy friends and family. While most photo booths rent for a minimum of $600, our customized DIY version is just a quarter of that cost, and rather than rent, you get to keep the photo printer for years to come.

Time Wise

The chalkboard takes about 3 hours to paint and dry. Assembly of the booth will take about 1 hour at the reception.

•

Divide & Conquer

While you can make the chalkboard frame ahead of time, the setup is most definitely a day-of wedding project and not something that the bridal party should handle. Hand this off to a trusted helper, several hours before the ceremony.

SUPPLIES

- Flat bed sheet, twin size or larger, depending on your space
- Crop-A-Dile tool or hole punch
- Removable adhesive hooks, 4 to 8, found at craft and hardware stores
- Picture frame, about 16 in. by 20 in.
- Chalkboard paint
- Chalk
- Digital camera with tripod
- Photo printer
- Scrapbook with blank pages
- Fine-point permanent marker
- Glue stick or double-sided tape

A.

B.

I love the addition of a photo frame-turned-chalkboard for a totally fresh and unique twist. You can also customize your booth by using different backdrops, adding props, and playing around with the lighting.

This project will take some effort and expense to pull together, so plan your timeline and budget accordingly.

DIRECTIONS

1. Let's get started by setting up your backdrop. Nearly any plain wall (without windows) will do as long as it's accessible to your guests, but out of the way of foot traffic and vendor entrances. An unused corner works great. Punch holes along the top edge of the sheet, about 1 in. from the top and 2 in. apart. Use these holes as a placement guide for when you attach the adhesive hooks to the wall.

2. Apply the hooks to the wall according to the manufacturer's instructions and hang the sheet on the hooks. You'll want the top of the sheet to hang high, at least 7 ft. from the ground. That way you won't see the top edge of the background behind any taller guests' heads.

3. On a nearby table close to an outlet, set up your camera, printer, and the scrapbook. Each camera and printer setup will be different, so check your operating manuals to determine what you'll need to get started with the electronics. The photo printer used for this project offers a preview of each shot from the camera and the ability to print only the shots you want (photo A).

4. For the photo frame chalkboard, remove the glass or plastic backing from a photo frame. Spray it (front and back) with two to three coats of chalkboard paint, and let it dry for at least 24 hours or per the manufacturer's instructions. Reinsert the glass or plastic, add some cardboard for backing, and you have a message-worthy chalkboard for your guests to write silly, fun, and poignant notes on that will then be seen when they take their turn in the photo booth.

Hours to go!

5. How does it all work? It's best to recruit a friend or two as photographers and printer monitors. This keeps the camera from walking away and helps keep wasteful shots and prints to a minimum. Have your bridal party spread the word that guests should stop by and have their photo taken. Print the photos and insert them into the scrapbook with double-sided tape or glue, and encourage the guests to leave a note of congrats to the happy couple in the scrapbook (photo B).

tips & hints

- *If you don't have a designated photographer, use a tripod. Add a note for guests on how to operate the self-timer.*

- *Not all venues will allow you to hang things on their walls. Ask your venue coordinator what their policy is before doing so. If hanging a backdrop is out, look for an unused corner of your venue and let the walls be the backdrop.*

- *Plain white backdrops can be too harsh to shoot against, but black backdrops are great for most shots. Think about using patterned sheets or fabrics that coordinate with your wedding theme. Feather boas and party hats are perfect props for your not-so-shy guests. And seating,*

like a little couch, stools, or chairs, is a great inclusion, too!

- *The booth area should be well lit, but not too bright, and well away from windows or doors.*

- *Be sure there's an electrical outlet near your photo booth location for the printer, any lighting you may add, and your battery charger. Bring an extension cord and surge protector or a power strip so your electricity needs are all taken care of, and have extra printer ink, batteries, extension cords, and USB cables on hand.*

- *For the scrapbook, have plenty of blank pages and pens available for guests to insert their photos and write notes to the newlyweds.*

Crafty Calculator

WHAT TO BUDGET

Twin sheet	$ 12.00
Removable hooks	$ 8.00
Photo printer	$ 100.00
Printer inks	$ 20.00
Photo frame	$ 16.00
Chalk paint	$ 5.00
Chalk	$ 1.00
Scrapbook	$ 15.00
Total	$ 177.00

COST COMPARISON

Commercial photo booth rentals cost upwards of $600.00 per evening. Our fully customizable version costs less than a third of that amount.

STORE COST	YOUR COST
$600.00	**$177.00**

Resources

Finding the right materials for your projects needn't be a stress-inducing task. I've put together this handy collection of places to find affordable supplies for the projects in this book, from general craft stores to fabric and flower shops to web sites for lace, ribbon, rubber stamps, paper crafts, and everything in between. Also check out my site, www.diybride.com, and my publisher's DIY community, www.CraftStylish.com.

General Craft Stores

A.C. Moore
www.acmoore.com

Jo-Ann Fabric and Craft Stores^{SM}
www.joann.com
Check them out for a wide and affordable selection of laces, buttons, and fabrics.

Michaels Stores^{SM}
www.michaels.com

Save-on-Crafts
www.save-on-crafts.com

Boxes

Paper Mart^{SM}
www.papermart.com

Paper Source^{SM}
www.paper-source.com

Fabric & Textiles

Denver Fabrics
www.denverfabrics.com
This website has a wide selection of textiles at very reasonable prices. Even with shipping costs, I found Denver to be more reasonable than many of my local sources.

Lartisana

www.lartisana.com
For lace or crochet doilies in a wide array of sizes and colors, I found this to be a fantastic resource.

Flowers

My wedding community at DIYBride.com raves about these online resources for flowers.

2G Roses
www.freshroses.com

Fifty Flowers
www.fiftyflowers.com

Flowerbud.com®
www.flowerbud.com

Grower's BoxSM
www.growersbox.com

Kelley Wholesale Florist
www.kelleywholesale.com

Garden Centers & Home Improvement Stores

Home DepotSM
www.homedepot.com
Their garden center is an excellent place to find interesting pots and containers for centerpieces and popcorn buffets.

Lowe'sSM
www.lowes.com

Rockler®
www.rockler.com
I found their selection of wood veneers to be excellent and affordable.

Graphic Images and Clip Art

ClipArt.Com™
www.clipart.com

iStockphoto®
www.istockphoto.com

Millinery Supplies

Judith M
www.judithm.com

Lacis
www.lacis.com
This is one of the best places in the United States to find unique laces and headbands.

Vintage Vogue
www.vintagevogue.com

Paper, Cardstock, and Envelopes

I have a mix of retailers and manufacturers in this category. While many manufacturers don't sell directly to the public, visit their websites to check out what's new and exciting in product offerings. They'll also usually have a list of retailer locations where you can find products. The retail shops I've included come highly recommended, and many have been reliable sources throughout my entire crafting career.

Action Envelope
www.actionenvelope.com

Bazzill Basics Paper, Inc.
www.bazzillbasics.com

Chatterbox, Inc.SM
www.chatterboxinc.com

Dick BlickSM
www.dickblick.com

Envelope Mall
www.envelopemall.com

Autumn Leaves®
www.autumnleaves.com

KI®**Memories, Inc.**
www.kimemories.com

Marco's Paper
www.marcopaper.com

My Mind's Eye
www.mymindseye.com

Paper Presentation
www.paperpresentation.com

Paper Source
www.paper-source.com

Pearl River
www.pearlriver.com

Stampin' Up!
www.stampinup.com

The Internet Wallpaper Store
www.wallpaperstore.com
This is one of the best sources for grass cloth wallpapers.

Ribbon

Great ribboneries abound online. Check out these fine retailers for beautiful, affordable ribbons in nearly every color and style imaginable.

Cheap Ribbons
www.cheapribbons.com

JKM Ribbons & Trim
www.jkmribbon.com

M & J Trimming
www.mjtrim.com

Of the Earth
www.custompaper.com

The Ribbon Spot™
www.theribbonspot.com

Rubber Stamps

Addicted to Rubber Stamps®
www.addictedtorubberstamps.com
A rubber stamp mega-store with thousands of rubber stamps.

Impress
www.impressrubberstamps.com
They have a great selection of fun and elegant stamps. They also have a very good selection of accessories, like brads and stickers, and they even make custom stamps.

Papertrey Ink
www.papertreyink.com

Savvy Stamps
www.savvystamps.com

Stampin' Up!
www.stampinup.com

The Memory Box®
www.memoryboxco.com

Vases & Glassware

Crate & Barrel®
www.crateandbarrel.com

eBay
www.ebay.com

IKEA®
www.ikea.com

Jamali Garden
www.jamaligarden.com

West Elm®
www.westelm.com

Index